T0195013

<u>Excerpts</u>

The biggest problem in life is discontentment, and greedy pursuit to find more spice for a life that has already been seasoned with salt.

My professor always told me to ignore what anybody else said about me so that I could go higher. He told me to prove myself, so that I would not point accusing fingers, without giving a solution to problems that nobody had ever solved. He told me to watch and see myself win. And guess what? I am still watching and win-ING. That is one of the prices that you must pay as a pacesetter.

In my life, I have a GOD who manages everything, sees everything, and just loves me the way I am. Then, some people do not see anything good in what you do. On the other hand, some people support you in everything you do. And some love to support you when you are down but are not too happy to see you excel. No matter where you are, and who you are with, it is better to know the bakers and butlers of your life (those who put the ingredients of your life together and open the doors of happiness and greatness for you to reach your destiny).

- Lessons from my kitchen

Lessons from my Kitchen

A MEMOIR

OLU LAOYE (MICAIAH)

LESSONS FROM MY KITCHEN
A MEMOIR

iUniverse books may be ordered through booksellers or by contacting:

iUniverse
1663 Liberty Drive
Bloomington, IN 47403
www.iuniverse.com
844-349-9409

Because of the dynamic nature of the Internet, any web addresses or links contained in this book may have changed since publication and may no longer be valid. The views expressed in this work are solely those of the author and do not necessarily reflect the views of the publisher, and the publisher hereby disclaims any responsibility for them.

Any people depicted in stock imagery provided by Getty Images are models, and such images are being used for illustrative purposes only. Certain stock imagery © Getty Images.

ISBN: 978-1-6632-3864-1 (sc)
ISBN: 978-1-6632-3865-8 (e)

Library of Congress Control Number: 2022907532

Print information available on the last page.

iUniverse rev. date: 04/29/2022

I dedicate this book to God, for letting me use my life as a lesson for others. And to the reader, who I hope will learn some things that may help them make good decisions.

Contents

Preface

It is a privilege to write the lessons of life, about life, in life, and for life. One of my biggest habits in college apart from singing and writing was cooking. I have always been a person who loves hosting guests. I like the idea of feeding lots of people anywhere I find myself. It does not matter where— Church, parties, dinners, on the streets, at my home. I just want to host guests and make them feel happy. There is something about having your loved ones around you in a festive environment. The cheers, the gests, the laughs, the music, dancing, food, prayers, encouragement, and the memories shared.

There is so much joy in togetherness, whenever people are in a certain place for the same reason, especially in a festive mood. There is a feeling of unity at that moment when you see your loved ones savoring the dishes that you spent hours preparing and complimenting you for a job well done. The music, the jokes, the "Oliver Twist" moments of asking for "just a little more" of the food, just gives me an attitude of gratitude. However, I must confess that the greatest lessons I have learned in life, came from my kitchen. I spent so much time in my kitchen alone, and I had the privilege of meditating about my life lessons, and even random thoughts on different philosophies, while I was cooking.

I must let you know that this is not a cookbook at all. I may briefly explain how I cook some dishes, but there are no food recipes in this book. I am only using my memories and thoughts about life issues that I kept in a journal when I randomly think about a food item or while cooking in the kitchen. This inspirational book contains some stories of my past: betrayal, food poisoning from a trusted person—an escape from a near-death experience, theft, embarrassments, astonishing surprises at the edge of disappointments, spiritual awakening to follow my dreams as I strived in tears— a story of accomplishments that were achieved by grace. I used all of these to explain some of the philosophies of life that I learned from the art of cooking a few dishes, and some of the lessons that I learned from different kinds of food items— I explained what they symbolize if I had to compare them to my life experiences.

Introduction

One of the greatest stories of my life was from my childhood. I remember one day when I was so hungry to a fault. I say my hunger was to a fault because I went to look for the food leftover in the refrigerator, but only found a little spoiled green soup (ewedu). It was spoiled to an extent of rotten smells since there was nobody at home to eat the food for many days. My grandparents and mother had gone to the hospital that morning, and I was the only one in the main house, while some other people were in the boys' quarters. Since I had never cooked anything at eight years old; and I was very hungry, I took a little cup of cassava flakes (Garri), and added some cold water to it, to make a mussel. Fortunately for me, my uncle's girlfriend walked into the kitchen, to find me getting set to eat the food. I will never forget the shocking fright on her face when she fearfully shouted: "What are you doing? Do you want to kill yourself"? I innocently explained to her, that I was only making Eba and Ewedu soup because I thought that is how our maids prepared it. I was devastated to see her throwing the spoilt food in the trash can, but quickly changed my attitude to a grateful one, when she cooked a delicious meal for me almost immediately. On that day, I decided to love cooking good food as much as I loved eating it.

For you to understand the reason for that story, let me introduce you to my background. During the early stage of my life, I lived in the southwestern region of Nigeria with my mother and grandparents. I was fortunate to live the aristocratic lifestyle— I mean the bourgeoisie kind of lifestyle. My grandfather was an ex-diplomat, and a Federal Character Commissioner, assigned by the late Gen. Sanni Abacha; my grandmother was a retired headmistress; my mom was an actress, and I was just a little spoiled brat living in my grandparents' house. For a little child like me, it felt good: all the attention, the maid, the nanny; the gardener; the security guards at our gate; and the chauffeur. I had everything I needed and more. It was a good life for a little girl like me. Then something unforgettable happened when I was eight years old. My mother fell ill. Shortly after, my maternal grandfather got hypertensive, and was diagnosed with diabetes; and my maternal grandmother also fell chronically ill. At eight years old, I had to make my own food sometimes. Thanks to my lovely mother who always made me spend more time learning from the nannies and doing house chores with them. Sooner or later, the maids left, and we had to survive. My strong mother still had to take care of herself even in sickness. I had to learn to do certain things like cleaning and cooking at this young age. I am grateful for the lessons that I learned from that time of my life because they shaped me into being a good cook, in addition to other talents.

A decade later, I spent more time in the kitchen during my teenage years in the university, because I started a business at eighteen years old called 'MamaGee Kitchen'. I started this business because I loved to cook for a lot of people in a certain big pot, and I felt it was a good idea to make money while I did what I loved as a college student. With the help of my generous friend, who bought me a big deep freezer and some foodstuff; and my mom who bought the other food items needed as well, I started advertising my food business, as I happily stumped Macy's to buy my first big pot. I started the business by cooking goat meat pepper soup, fish pepper soup, red stew with rice and plantains. To my surprise, many people patronized me. They kept coming back, and some even drove over forty miles to eat my food. The business was so lucrative that I did not have to get a second job as an undergraduate student for almost two years. I cooked for a guest-size range of single customers to house parties, and even to a size of up to one hundred and fifty people for Church potluck.

Since I spent most of my time in the kitchen, I was able to think deeply about many issues of life, and the philosophy of solving problems that they bring. Like a scientist who spends most of their time in a lab with a rabbit that was locked in a cage for scientific study and research, I found some interesting attributes in the issues of life in relation to some food items and even some art of cooking a few dishes. Some of the topics that I talked about were issues that we go through daily in our life—for example, I compared underestimating people who turned out to be greater than us in the future, to jollof rice. I compared betrayal to draw soup, and I compared baking bread to destiny helpers and mentors. In this book, I narrated some personal experiences that taught me great lessons for the reader to learn about the life, as they look through the lens of my kitchen.

1

My Jollof Life Story

I come from a peculiar and very interesting country, Nigeria. I am so proud to be a Nigerian American, and I will not trade it for anything— well, except Christ. In Nigeria, we celebrate everything in a big way. You celebrate your birthday, spouse introduction, traditional wedding, church wedding, wedding anniversary, christening, promotion, retirement, ordination, a celebration of gaining admission into a university, graduation, housewarming, music album launch, book launch, new business opening, new church opening, funeral, even a dead person's remembrance. I mean, we just like to party.

There is a food item that must be served at your party and is the most compulsory item you must budget for while planning your bash. It is the world's greatest and most popular 'Jollof Rice'. We argue that Nigeria has the tastiest jollof rice in the world, amongst other African countries. There is always a great debate between Ghana and Nigerians, about the country that has the most delicious Jollof, and I predict this argument would end when Jesus comes back. This story is for another day.

The jollof rice is a combination of rice, tomatoes, tomatoes paste, onions, peppers, chicken broth, and other seasonings. It is the most sort-after dish at any celebration, and we can never get tired of it. We eat it with chicken, beef, fish, shrimp, vegetables, plantain, salad, etc. It is one of the best dishes that I ever learned to cook at a young age, and I love cooking it for many people at the same time. My family loves eating it, and I love hearing their compliments repeatedly after they have devoured a very palatable plate of Jollof.

I have come to learn some lessons from cooking jollof rice, which I would be discussing in this book as secrets to my success through the philosophy of life. Jollof rice is cooked by frying tomato sauce with onions and peppers, and then adding parboiled rice to the fried sauce, while it is steaming. You must stir the rice with the sauce mixture, giving it an orange or reddish look—hence, the name 'Jollof'. The finished product is always tasty to eat with chicken or other meats or seafood. We usually joke that the rice at the surface of the pot, is not as tasty as the rice at the bottom, so the quickest fix to it is that you pour the whole content of the pot in a cooler or foil pan, especially during parties and get-together celebrations. What I learned from this easy fix, is that the rice at the bottom of the pot ends up at the top of the cooler. The rice at the bottom of a pot endures much more heat from the gas cooker than the rice at the top; thus, absorbing much more ingredients, flavor, and color.

Is not that what we go through at the end of our struggles? Whenever we go through the struggles of life, we feel that the heat is too much to endure. We are unable to cope with the pain, which threatens to drain us to death. We get so hopeless at times, that we tend to compare the efforts of those at the top with ours, but we refuse to realize that our struggles and battles increase the succulence and flavor of our personality. Just like the softness of the jollof rice at the bottom of the pot, we come out with a better attitude, full of compassion and mercy for those who are struggling. We speak with more intelligence and edifice. We give life to the little things that people receive from us, leaving lasting memories through the testimony of our heat, and leaving lasting impacts in people's hearts as they remember conversations. I have come to realize that the most impactful sermons and inspirational talks that I have listened to are those that were spoken by people who went through so many hard times, that their struggles were life-changing. You cannot deliver a testimony if you do not go through a test. Are you enduring the heat of the pot with the hope that you will succeed someday soon, and you will use your lessons to change the world? Or are you using the lessons learned to push people away from you, because you want them to go through the same struggles that you had to endure? Are you dwelling at the bottom of the pot for a longer time till your rice burns in bitterness, where others will not be able to get value from your life anymore? You attract what you give out. If your testimony does not edify but rather gives your friends and family more stress and sadness, you will attract that to yourself as well. You need to learn to use every opportunity that you have, to show an attitude of gratitude from every testimony; and draw people closer to their creator by giving Him Glory.

There is this story that I hate to tell for two reasons: it makes me regret underestimating somebody, and it is almost unbelievable but true. Some years ago, before I ever thought of going into music professionally, I was Facebook friends with a young man who was trying to break into the music industry. He knew that I was quite familiar with a few people in the public relations industry, and I knew a few Africans in the United States, who were either DJs or recording artists, or promoters. He reached out to me on Facebook instant messaging several times to introduce himself to me as an upcoming artist, but I ignored him because I felt I could not help him, since I had so much schoolwork that was overwhelming at that time, coupled with the fact that I just didn't want to make friends overseas. Perhaps, I could have done the due diligence of courtesy to respond to his message, and try to encourage him by referring him to a few people. Better still, I could have even shared his song on my Facebook profile for people to listen to. But I was going through so much stress emotionally in my own life, that I hardly responded to strangers sending me messages on Facebook. A year later, he was found by somebody else in Nigeria that helped him get a record label contract. He released his first song, and he got popular.

Over the next decade, he released more songs and became so famous that he started collaborating with international artists, he became one of the biggest stars in the continent of Africa and is well known outside the continent too, with many awards to his name. Of course, like most celebrities, he deleted his original Facebook account and set up a new one.

We are no more Facebook friends, but I am very happy every time I hear of his success. Since I ignored him in the days of his little beginnings, I do not expect him to remember me now that he is successful. Even if he does, it would be to thank God that he achieved stardom and wealth in music, despite the number of rejections from many people like me. I remember this story most times, especially when I think of how the jollof rice at the bottom of a pot will surely end up at the top of the cooler. Though I do not need his help with my music because we sing entirely different genres, I could have been a friend to someone who pushed through all odds to succeed on earth.

So, you may wonder why I included this story in my book. I wanted to illustrate this scenario by pointing to the repercussions of those decisions that we choose to make, just because we feel 'too good. It has changed me a lot, and it is still changing me to see everybody as God sees them. We are all different and unique in the talents that we exhibit, and nobody has the right to see themselves better than you.

I have heard many stories of students who were mocked for coming from the poorest families in a classroom, but they grew up to be the richest men and women amongst their peers. In most cases, they do not go back to make their former classmates sad, but they show grace in the way they communicate with them, and they end up being more admirable.

Have you ever gone back to visit the old job that you left ten years ago? How do you feel when you see the same tough supervisor that gave you a headache at all times, still working at the same job with little raise in all those years—while you are making over three times his or her salary? Does it make you smile, and just give God praise? Or do you say something to spite the boss, and cause them to regret it? The first option of gratitude with a smile always wins the case because you do not need to say negative things to make people regret their actions, especially when you already won the battle. A battle-winner does not waste time smiting others with vengeful words but instead shows grace in the sweetness of their attitude. I can conclude that this analogy about the jollof rice, is the reason why the Jollof at the bottom of the pot is usually more delicious than the one at the top, making it a valid reason to turn the rice from the pot into a cooler. When you turn the rice from pot to cooler, the Jollof at the bottom automatically becomes the one at the top and vice versa. Even when we use a spoon to stir the rice for an even taste, the top is still the most delicious, because it does not produce the bitterness of the heat that it endured.

I have noticed that people may not remember everything that you said, but your actions of grace to those who hurt you in the past will continue in their memories for a lifetime. The irony of life is that we tend to pour out wisdom to people who may not desire the wise lessons that we have to offer until we have gone through so much heat, and we realize that we do not need to dish out our advice to those who do not need it. It is important to use our lessons to touch the lives of others, but we should choose our audience wisely after a test— like the jollof rice meets the satisfaction of those who can endure the heat and spice. Is your audience willing to handle the heat of their test with the strategies that your advice gives them? Will they use the flavor and spice from their lessons to touch the lives of others as well, or will they keep it like the burnt part of the pots that may not be palatable? You must use your experience to not only preach a testimony but mentor your listeners until they use the valuable strategies of your lesson in their own tests. That is how you can practically bring value to others. Your responsibility in transforming lives is not necessarily by social media influencer pages or music or drama. Your responsibility is the visible product of your encouragement in the lives of those you see every day, and your followers in all places—social media and real-life outside the internet.

2

Efo Riro— My Green Vegetable Lesson

One of my favorite dishes to cook in the kitchen is the Nigerian vegetable soup. It is a mixture of either spinach, collard greens, or kale in a cooked stew that contains a blend of tomatoes, onions, peppers, and spices. I like to blend the tomatoes, onions, and peppers in a coarse texture, and then cook it in heated palm oil; then I add different boiled meats, poultry, and seafood with the broth used to boil the meat, salt, and bouillon cubes. After the blended stew fries, I add any choice or mixture of spinach, boiled collard greens that I drained, or kale to the stew. Then I allow the whole soup to cook until the vegetables are soft and edible. When the soup is fully cooked, we eat it with cooked rice, fufu, or alone. In my culture, we believe the richness of this soup is determined by the number of spices, meats, and seafood included in the soup.

The variety of condiments added to this dish will determine the flavor of the rich dish, but also determines the nutritional value of the dish.

I learned a few lessons from cooking this vegetable soup, and I appreciate the knowledge that we could get from analyzing the recipe and comparing it to our daily lives. The first lesson is the heated palm oil. Only a heated palm oil can fry the blended tomatoes, onions, and peppers to the desired taste. The blended mix is in a coarse texture because it determines the taste of the soup with the condiments. I don't know about you, but I know that I have been able to provide the flavorful spice in my talents to the world when I had experienced the heat of certain conditions. Like some people, I noticed that I get into a heated situation whenever I do not smoothen my ways or habits, and the intensity of that hot training to amend my steps has made me come out as pure gold. After I have emerged as a valuable product, many condiments will be added to beautify me as the nutritious product that the world needs. This brings me to the assortments that are added to the fried stew, which are the meats and seafood. The meats are usually boiled in water and spices with onions, to give flavor. The boiled meat must be soft and palatable, with the broth used as the seasoning for the vegetable soup. This teaches me that you need to make valuable and seasoned friends after you come out of the fire. If the meat is not deliciously ready to be added to the vegetable soup, it will deter the value that the chef anticipates. This is also the same for someone who is coming out of a negative situation and the lessons of life, with the desire to add value and gain more. If you emerge as pure gold after a tribulation, you need to affiliate with those who are not willing to judge you but are willing to add a more positive impact on your life.

The main ingredient of this dish is spinach or boiled collard greens, or kale. However, this is the last ingredient added to cook the dish, because it should only be mixed with the previously added ingredients and left to simmer to absorb the flavor of the stew for a few minutes. I asked myself why it takes only a few minutes for the main ingredients to stay on the fire, unlike the others. I realized that the other ingredients had already gone through the heat to absorb each other's flavors, and all that is needed is a few more minutes for the main ingredient to be added to simmer. When you take care of the root of your life, you will be able to have a simpler solution to whatever goals that you set for yourself or problems that you are facing. For example, your family tradition, your beliefs, your relationships, and the training that you were given by your parents from a young age, are all big contributors to the end product of your life. If you are not at peace with your foundation or identity, you cannot show the world a character for others to emulate.

We all know one of the richest sources of protein is spinach. The spinach excretes its nutrients into any soup, to make a melody with the seasoning for great taste. How many nutrients and values can you give to people who come into your life to season it? Do you invite them with the spice of comfort; or do you fight them with a rotten and bitter product of your painful pasts or memories. We boil the spinach sometimes and drain the water before adding it to the soup mixture, because there is a belief that the impurities will be cleansed from raw spinach, and this would prevent us from purging or defecating at frequent times per day, due to our consumption of the dish.

Are you like the spinach that has been boiled and drained, so that you can still produce a positive impact on those who you encounter? The truth is that you are the only one who can answer that question when you have a reflection on how you react to the people around you.

3

Draw Soup
(The Draw-Back People)

need to start this chapter with a synopsis of a 'seasonal friend'. I know I have one of them. I think one of the reasons why I am writing this, is because I am baffled by the behavior of people who think they are smart enough to outwit other people, and they end up getting stuck in their mess. Unfortunately, when they are in the mess that they caused for themselves, they are too ashamed to go back to those that they shadily thought they had outsmarted in the past. It always happens that those are the people who get to suffer consequences that they regretfully admit could have been avoided. A perfect example is a friend that I know, who always runs to me for help when they have shadily treated others unfairly, but they would disappear into thin air when you need their own help. It happened so many times, that I honestly think I will keep a notepad, just to write the dates of the various occurrences; and when the "crook" comes back after a while in shambles, I will gladly show them their mess. Don't judge me, you would do the same. These kinds of people are the ones that you could empty your bank account for, but they will not show up when you are in a crisis or in need at the hospital. They feel that they are smart to come to beg you for food or money or a job recommendation, or even a letter as a witness in court, but they go right away to scam other friends after you help them. Yes, forgive them for your sanity; but shut those people out and keep your help to yourself, when you notice that they are intentionally doing the same thing to take you for a fool too many times. They will keep doing it repeatedly until you point out their insanity. They draw you back from the direction that you are going because you could have used your resources to groom your own life and accomplish positive goals for yourself. I relate their behavior to the draw soup.

When I was young, I used to like the 'Okra soup', which is a combination of diced okras and salt that have been cooked in boiling water. We would usually eat it with red tomato and pepper stew with meats or seafood. After some years, I started liking the sophisticated style of cooking this Okra in the blend of pureed tomatoes, peppers, seafood, and meats. The joy of eating this dish with any swallow is the slimy nature of the soup while you are taking it from the dish into your mouth. It draws like slime, and its quality is judged by how slimy it gets when you are drawing it from the cooking pot to your plate. Hence, the name 'draw soup' was given to it. There is another type of Nigerian soup that could be categorized as a 'draw soup'. It is known as 'Ogbono'. This soup is made with the wild-African-mango seeds (Ogbono). I cook it with very heated and bleached palm oil so that the granulated seeds will be slimy when it is added to the extremely heated palm oil. I then add more hot water gradually, until the soup rises to an ample amount. I finally add seasoning and meats with seafood and leave it to simmer till well done. However, I do not cover the pot at all when cooking any draw soup, because I have grown with the mentality that the soup will not draw nor get slimy when you cover it.

Isn't that how life is, with those people that draw you back from your goals? They are intentional; noisy, and usually have a self-pity attitude for public display. They want to make sure you see that they are in misfortune, and make you feel that you are the only one that can save them. It is smart to immediately point out that they are intentionally manipulating your niceness, even though they know that they can run to other people to tell the same cock and bull stories that they told you. They see an opportunity to fool you if you do not promptly tell them that only God can help them, not you. Do not try to be the savior of the world with manipulators, because they are only playing with your sense by using their lies. It is wise to help people with reason, and not after manipulative pleadings. They are like the okra soup, whose slime can be disrupted by twisting your hand while it is drawing/slimy, as you serve it from the pot; and as you eat it from your plate. I have learned to disrupt manipulative relationships with those who think they are too witty and too smart to be caught. I call them slimy opportunists. Once again, do not judge me.

Another group of people that I categorize as the "draw soup" are the obvious antagonists. They are noticeably clear about the fact that they see you trying to climb the ladder of success, but they do not believe you deserve it—even though you are highly talented, passionate, and hardworking. They come to you in the form of friends at times, when you feel so comfortable telling them your dreams, goals, and aspirations. They know in their hearts that you can achieve all these, but they feel intimidated by your planned success. They are usually the first set of people that draw you back from the plans that you had previously set, by giving you a "thousand and one" reasons why they think that you are not good enough. They are the 'naysayers' to every idea that you have, but they carefully listen to your plans to steal the ideas from you and run off to make a fortune in their own name. If you have not met people like that in the past, be careful of them in the future. The best way to avoid circumstances such as these is to lay your plans in prayer before God and ask Him to lead you to the clean-hearted people who will guide you in the right direction until you reach your goal. It always works for me, and I believe it will work for anyone who does this too.

My last set of the "draw soup" people are those who just do not like you, don't care much about your existence, or might like you but not your style. I will give you a perfect example. I am humbled to let you know that I am a Christian recording artist, who writes the majority of my songs in English and my native language (Yoruba). I remember the first time that I released my debut album which was titled 'Tani t'Oluwa', which means "Who is like our God". Many people supported me to my surprise, and I am grateful for my friends and family because they made noise about it everywhere. My Nigerian lovers also shared my songs everywhere and encouraged me both at home and abroad.

I was more astonished at my big non-Nigerian fan base, and the testimony of my American friends, bosses, coworkers, and others. I started getting messages from people in far North and East Africa, who said that they watched my music videos from their country. As if that was not enough, some people from the United Kingdom sent messages to me and told me that they loved my music. However, there were some "Nigerians" who thought it was "appallingly non-appropriate" to release an album in my native language, because I live in the United States, and nobody would like to "hear or speak" Yoruba. They even refused to buy my CDs for a reason like that. Some of them shrugged off the idea of inviting me to sing at their gatherings or concerts, because my style was not acceptable to them, and I do not sing strictly "English songs as they do". It did not bother me, because I got a call from a large African American Baptist Women's group in the United States, and they asked me to sing as a guest at their Convention. They requested only my native songs, and I was so dumbfounded for a few moments.

That was the first largest audience that ever performed for. I was more surprised to see some of them writing some words I sang in the songs and remarking about the meanings that I mentioned on stage. We had so much fun, and I wouldn't trade it for anything. This story is not to proudly narrate my accomplishment, because I know that I haven't accomplished a lot in life yet; but I used this story to encourage you by letting you know that there are people out there, who are looking for someone exactly like you to bless them with the gifts and talents that you have, in your style. You will just have to pray, as you patiently wait for them to find you. Sometimes, it takes some actions like introducing yourself to them. Go for it because I am cheering you on!

4

The Bakers

I n my life, I have a GOD who manages everything, sees everything, and just loves me the way I am. Then, some people do not see anything good in what you do. On the other hand, some people support you in everything you do. And some love to support you when you are down but aren't too happy to see you excel. No matter where you are, and who you are with, it is better to know the bakers and butlers of your life (those who put the ingredients of your life together and open the doors of happiness and greatness for you to reach your destiny). My next two chapters will explain the importance of having both the bakers of your life and the butlers. But this chapter concentrates on the bakers—those who put the ingredients of your life together, to make it a delicious piece of value to the world, like a three-layer chocolate cake or a mouthwatering vanilla yogurt cake.

When I was in graduate school, I learned how to make yogurt cake. I got so addicted to it, that I could eat a whole pan if I was given the chance. My friend from the Republic of Côte d'Ivoire taught me to use flour, sugar, eggs, baking powder, butter, and vanilla yogurt to bake this cake. I did not have to add milk to it, but I still added my milk to the recipe, just to give it a little creamier taste. This recipe reminds me of so many things that people have noticed as gifts in my life, and they aligned their observations to influence me in using my talents today.

The art of baking has influenced this reminisce on some of my experiences as a child, and how they contributed to my adult life. I grew up spoiled but also groomed by a very sweet but principled mother and loving maternal grandparents. My dear mother pampered me by taking me to different countries in the summer. In addition to the lovely holidays, my grandfather always bought me candy and cookies every single day. I remember my little legs running every evening to the gate, once I hear my grandpa's car horn which announced his arrival from work. My grandfather would open his car door to put me on his lap as the gateman opens the gate for him to enter our compound, and we will drive down through the gate to park his car. Now that I think about it, my little hands were placed on the steering wheel for me to assume that I was the driver of the car, but it was my grandfather that was using his own skilled hands to drive the car safely till we parked it. It is funny how I must have felt like an expert driver, not knowing that someone else was doing the job.

When I was a small girl, I used to write songs because I spent time with my maternal grandmother, who loved to formulate songs in her head whenever she read the Bible. She would sit me on her bed, and then sing to me. She would also sit in the living room on most evenings, and she would tell me African tales which had songs in them. She saw something in me that I had not noticed— music is my life, my calling, my passion, my hideout, my solution, my joy, and my first love. I loved to sing in front of the television at night when everybody gathered to watch the evening news. I knew that was the only time that everyone gathered, and I wanted them to hear me sing. My grandfather who was highly committed to the news due to his governmental position was loving enough to let me stay there and sing, even though it was distracting him from the news. Now that I am grown, I often remember my grandparents for this love. They saw the passion at a young age but never lived long to see me on the same television stations that I used to distract them from.

On the day I saw my first music video on the African Independent Television, I remembered my daily practice of singing aloud in front of the television when the newscaster was reading the news on that same television station. Of course, I never knew that I would be on that same television about two decades after, but I knew that I loved to be seen singing passionately as a young girl. I owe gratitude to my mother for taking the music to some of the television stations that I distracted my whole family's attention from, just to remind me that 'my dream has come through. Back then at my young age, my grandparents saw just the flour and sugar of a little girl, but many other people had to add more ingredients within two decades for me to deliver the cake to the world.

I went to primary school and was taught to play the flute for just a little while. I fell in love with music so much that I joined the school chorale group. We were often invited to sing at different events, and I loved the feeling of performing for people. I loved the instruments so much that I asked my aunty in the United Kingdom to kindly send me a keyboard for my birthday gift. I was so excited when she sent it to me a few months later, but I am so sad that I did not get to learn how to play the keyboard to date. In those days, it was not common to have private keyboard lessons, compared to private school lessons for mathematics and English language classes, that I was enrolled in.

I went to secondary school shortly after, and I forgot about the keyboard lessons for the six years that I was at the school. However, I remained in love with music. Many people knew that I loved to sing, and I will never forget a certain day when my singing talent saved me from being punished with other people. I went to a boarding school for my secondary education, and we had a lot of experiences in the Jungle which I narrated some of them in Chapter 8. One of the very harsh situations was the mass punishment of junior students by senior students when something goes wrong. All the junior students in the dormitory could spend several minutes or even an hour, serving the punishment of one person's sin—especially if the culprit does not confess that they committed the offense, and the senior students do not know who committed the atrocity. Even on very few occasions, a wicked senior could call all junior students, and punish them for no reason.

One day, a senior called all the junior students to serve punishments in my dormitory, and she told us all to kneel and raise our hands. Then she changed the punishment to staying in press-up positions. To my surprise, she told me to stand up and sing and dance for the other junior students as they kept serving their punishment. I had no choice but to obey her, and I kept singing to entertain until the punishment was over. Though I was in the state of doing what I loved to do to entertain other people, I was able to feel their pain as they cried while serving the punishments. I think this has taught me to put my emotions into my music, and it molded me to start writing songs even when I am in pain. Sometimes, the senior calls me to sing for her because she liked to hear my voice. I still see that experience as a medium that prepared me for the future. Though the senior student did not know that she was being used by God to prepare me for a future in professional music. I got an email from her a few days ago, about how proud she was of me. She did not know that I eventually became a recording artist, until when she coincidentally saw my video on YouTube. I reminded her of our high school, but she forgot all about it. Though she forgot, I remembered and thanked her for being a "Baker" in my life, even though she did so unconsciously.

I remember one of my schoolteachers who had a dream about me in secondary school, and he responded to that dream by buying me a Christian book to help me grow spiritually; he asked me to read it. I also attribute this act of my teacher, as a positive move to preparing my future as a baker in my life. I later started leading a band of first-year junior students when I got to my first year in senior secondary school. We called it the JSS1 band, and it was the most entertaining on Sundays during students' church service. I taught the juniors new songs and helped them to use their talents in music, with their voice and instruments. My passion for music never left until I graduated secondary school because I was able to use the gifts that I had, to please God and people.

5

The Butlers

I cannot emphasize how grateful I am to the people who selflessly opened doors for me as a little immigrant in the United States, to accomplish some of my goals. They taught me that I would gain much satisfaction when I help other people rise in their journey of life. They have been so encouraging and never asked for anything in return for the goodness that they have shown me— in parenting, mentorship, guidance, education, finances, ministry, music, jobs, business, and so many other things. They are the ones that I call the "butlers" of my life's journey because they open the doors of happiness and greatness for me to reach my destiny. I also call them destiny-helpers sent by God.

We all need butlers in our lives because they help us get to our desired destination easier and effectively. I say effectively, because they prepare you for everything you may encounter in the place where you desire to reach, and they train you by carrying you closely like their own special project— some even invest so much energy in polishing you just like their own child. You are very lucky and blessed to have a mentor who advises you positively, and never judges you nor underestimates you for your inexperience. They do not laugh at your questions nor talk down on you to discourage your ambition —most especially when they have many decades of experience in your dream path. They let you know you are just fine, even when you doubt yourself. The best thing is to give God some magnificent praise for having them. It is good to be mentored by someone who knows and understands the intricacies of your journey because they are more capable of directing you through the process of getting to the peak.

In this chapter, I will be writing about recognizing butlers and choosing some of them to channel you to your expected end. I will also point out characteristics that could help you mentor some people too, as you try to add value to their lives.

I have been able to accomplish some of the things in my life because I have enjoyed the privilege of having some selfless mentors that I call 'legendary angels'. These amazing people have kicked me to study hard; yelled at me to sing loud; pushed me to write in academia; practically pestered me to release some projects that will outlast my own life, and held me accountable for all my actions until today. Do not feel bad if you ask someone to mentor you, and they refuse or they do not respond at all. Everyone goes through rejection, but we all find that mentor that will do anything to break walls for you to finally get to the peak of your success. Unfortunately, there are some people that I thought could mentor me, but they refused to do so because they do not know if they could train me to be where I had dreamed to be—I appreciate their honesty in responding to my request in this way.

I have compiled a few things that I have included on my checklist, every time that I consider someone as my mentor. Some of them could help you as well, while you pursue your dream of being mentored by a legend.

1. Look NOT for money, BUT reputation. Your mentor should not necessarily be a billionaire or a multimillionaire but should be someone whose work has produced good outcomes with proof of work. Anybody that tells you that they did not lift a finger to get rich, has no business being your mentor. The principle of life is that you work and get paid for your wages—it can never be "sit and do nothing, but money will come." You have to do something to get something: pray, study, learn, and work.

2. Learn from somebody with good character. Your hard work could take you to a great place, but your character will keep you in that successful place where you find yourself. You may think that successful people are needed by everybody, and they do not need to have good behavior. But a wise successful person usually considers portraying good behavior in their lifestyle—respectful communication; considerate behavior; humble mannerism; prudent spending; and a disciplined principle with habits that people want to emulate. They know that: if you are going to write a story, it should better be an interesting and lesson-filled one that will be commended a century later, just like it had always been. This is like the stories of many

prestigious people of the past that I have read, and I use the lessons from their life experiences to address some important decisions that I had to make.

3. Look for someone who has foresight. A leader should be able to recognize the season that you are in and must wisely detect the direction to lead you through with discretion. Your mentor should not be someone who just 'goes with the flow.' This makes me remember that "the blind cannot lead the blind, because they would both fall into a pit"—the only mentor that goes with the flow has not considered the saying. Choose a person who understands the trends of the world and the changes that you should be mindful of so that you can diligently work to avoid future challenges.

4. Choose to model someone who is quick to take responsibility for their actions and make amends if there are any mistakes. This should be someone who does not shy away from telling you about the mistakes they made, and the process they took to correct them. It will help to build your experience in determining decisions to make in your own life.

5. Choose someone who has focus. It is very important to have a mentor who sets goals and will not allow any distraction to deter their efforts to reach these goals. I cannot stress how easy your life could be if you are led by someone who intentionally strives to always be at the right place at the right time.

I have seen some people who intentionally go to the wrong place at the right time, but they end up regretting it for the rest of their lives. For example, some people go on an excessive shopping spree during tax-free weekends, for things that they do not even need; meanwhile, they had the option of attending a young entrepreneurs' conference that they previously scheduled, which had shown them prospects of profitable business opportunities if they attended it. The shopping spree during tax-free weekends is not wrong, it is actually a right place; but the time was wrong because they went shopping for things that were not as useful to them, which made them miss a scheduled seminar that could have changed their lives and businesses for the rest of their lives.

Some people really go to the right place at the wrong time, but they end up wasting their resources at that period, by not getting any profit from it. For example, some people see a trend of small business opportunity in selling products in a pyramid business which seemed lucrative for other people, so they also copy that trend and invest in it. However, they do not make any money in that business because they never had experience in the business yet. They did not get enough training and experience in the business, and they did not build a clientele that was necessary for their sales before they started the business. So, they end up in a loss that could have been easily avoided, if they stayed in their original business of styling people's hair—which used to bring them a monthly income of $10,000 per month.

There is a need for clear discernment in the business ideas that you pick, not a prediction of profit based on how you think other people are getting their returns over their investments. For example, the fact that your friend is getting rich from a business does not mean you should copy that business idea. You cannot gain from copying a friend's business model by calculating their profits, because you are not your friend; you do not have your friend's character; you do not have your friend's experience in totality; neither are you a clone of your friend. Get your idea and build on it.

6. Look for someone who does not love money above humans. If you want to be mentored by someone who is extremely money-hungry, be ready to be used by them to your detriment. They will turn you into their servant, without teaching you anything, neither will they pay you—so you will end up losing on both sides because you have gained nothing, but the mentor has stolen your ideas to build their own empire, and they have made you serve them for no pay. No matter how rich a person is, study their mannerism toward money. An extreme lover of money does not mind killing somebody else for money. An extreme money-lover already knows how much they will gain from you from the first conversation that you have with them, but they do not have plans for how to change your life positively. An extreme money-lover will never allow you to get to your great destiny free of charge, and they will continue to remind you that they made you famous—so they will keep asking for favors, and they always feel entitled to getting paid with several

favors at your detriment. Be careful of who you choose because there are wolves among lambs.

7. Look for Integrity. Cherish integrity. If a mentor has no integrity, they could disappoint you. A person whose "no" is "NO" will guide you in transparency, throughout your journey in life with them. A person with integrity will be always honest with you and cannot falter their relationship with you. They will not encourage you in person like a hypocrite and then turn around to talk negatively about you in your absence. A person with integrity sees your vulnerability, and will not use it against you, but can support you by guiding you through the correct paths until you are good enough. It is left to you to continue to build yourself after that mentorship for the rest of your own life. However, they will not leave you struggling, until they are sure that you are comfortable.

8. Look for a mentor that will train you to be a mentor to others. I do not know about anyone else, but I would prefer to be trained by someone who believes that I can help other people to become successful. Does your mentor see you as a leader that just needs to be trained to exhibit that leadership trait? Does your mentor train you to teach others how to lead, by showing an exemplary lesson? Do you feel that your potential mentor treats you like a leader already, by letting you see yourself through their lens? If your answer to all these remains a 'no', then that mentor may not be the best for you. The fact that someone is a billionaire does not mean that they can teach you to be a successful leader.

Even if you see someone being praised on television or social media, or you see them winning a Grammy award, they may not be your best choice for mentorship if they do not believe that you could be as successful as they are, by leading you and teaching you in advance to lead others that you will mentor in future—the continuity in the lessons that you learned from your mentor is the legacy that this mentor left for you, and the other people you will train.

9. Look for a mentor who does not only seek your success but seeks the well-being of your soul. Try to find someone who looks out for your mental wellness; guides the steps that you take to keep your internal circle and family loved and cared for; sees the things that may wear you out in times of desperation; and will go out to find you solutions for it.

10. I love to pray before I make important decisions like choosing someone else to direct me. Your mentor could determine the circumstances that you experience for the rest of your life because you will adapt a lot of their philosophies and ideology. If the mentor is not right for you, you could make a lot of mistakes based on the decisions you believed were best for long-term choices. I believe that God knows your heart, and He knows the best person who can lead you in the right way. Prayers always work for this, because I do not believe that I can do it all on my own.

6

Fry The Rice (Fried Rice)

There is a dish that I love to cook a lot because it is easy, and it takes much less time than a lot of other Nigerian dishes. It is also very colorful, and I do not know if I can get enough of it every time. It is called fried rice, and I think it was named fried rice because we parboil the rice and fry it in vegetable oil, marinated mixed vegetables, seasonings, diced bell peppers, with curry and thyme. Some people add shrimp, diced beef, and/or chicken livers to the mixture that is to be fried with the rice. It is one of the most colorful dishes that we have in West Africa, and I compliment the mixed vegetables and diced peppers for the elegance and beauty portrayed.

One day, I thought of the contribution of mixed vegetables in the Nigerian fried rice, and I wondered if most people would still eat it if the dish had no mixed vegetables of different colors. The nutritional value of the vegetables is not forgotten, but the beauty of the colors in the fried rice mainly contributes to its attraction. People are attracted to you for the life that you give in your manners to them. If you produce color and happiness when they are communicating with you, they will keep coming back for more.

There was a time in my life when I thought that everything was just going wrong for me. I lost a lot of people and things; I lost friends and lost lovers; I lost my sanity; I lost vision; I lost some family members; and I lost my zeal and passion for music. It was so bad that sometimes I just felt I could not even spell my name correctly anymore; I didn't want to speak to anybody, nor did I want to hear any music. I think if anybody knew me, they would know that I live with music every single moment of my life. I wanted to turn away from everything and everybody because I was so depressed and full of regrets about the actions of my past that contributed to the future which I might not be able to change.

But then as time went on, I spent a lot of time reading the Bible and studying the word of God in prayer. He told me that nobody can change my mood or my feelings, except if I give them the power to do so. I needed to accept my inability to be the commander of the whole universe and stop trying to change situations beyond my control. He told me that he is the only one that controls everything in heaven and earth, and I do not have any power to change how he turns situations for His glory. But it did show me that everything I am going through is for my good. He told me that he allowed me to lose friends so that I would know the true friends that he has blessed me with; he allowed me to lose a job that he knew could take my life; he allowed me to drift away from the hobbies that I thought were making me happy because they did not allow me to spend time with him as much as I should have been doing. But He also let me know that the love that I have for my music will never go away except if I let it go because he has given me an irrevocable anointing that nobody can take away from me except if I want to throw it away.

He also let me know that on the day of judgment we will all be accountable for how we have spent the talents that he has given to us on earth— have we been able to use our talents to encourage each other, or to save lives of people that thought that they could not make any good thing out of their own lives? Have we been able to use our talents to praise Him, or even if we are not in the Christian or gospel ministry, have we been able to use our talents to sing emotional and passionate love songs for couples that were at the breach of breaking their homes in a divorce? Have we been able to use our talents to help little children that are vulnerable in places where nobody cares about them, and to make them know that there is a better future for them? I broke down! "NO, I've not done enough!" I responded. He told me to add color to the life that he has given me, by writing a vision and making it plain according to Habakkuk 2: 2 (King James Version), which says:

> "And the LORD answered me, Write the vision, and make it plain upon tables, that he may run that readeth it."

He told me that he is the author and finisher of my faith and my life, and he has given me so much to do for the rest of my life, that even if I do not have anybody else to support me or to give me anything, I would still work with my talent for his glory. He told me that he has blessed me with so much wealth in skills and a voice, also with compassion and a vibrant lifestyle. He told me that many people do not know what I am going through because when they see me, they see only a lively and jovial person who does not show that she is going through a whole lot of mess. He said that he is going to allow them to see me that way because nobody needs to know a problem that they cannot solve for me— since he remains my own personal Lord and Savior. But he told me something that I will hold onto, and I will live by it for the rest of my life as my standard. He told me to show that same vibrant and colorful lifestyle of mine in the songs that I write, and I would see how people will react to them. So, I got up and started strategizing on what to do to make a more colorful life for myself, since this enlightened me to see that I have the power to change my mentality.

I changed the downcast behavior by first jumping out of the bed which I used as my 'pity-party crying venue'. Then I started an intentional to-do list for daily planning, toward a productive day every morning. Next, I cooked more often— cooking is a way of relaxation for me because I can get new ideas and plan on them, or sometimes I do other things like meditating on God's word as He communicates with me while I cook in the kitchen, or on other times when I think of different philosophies or ideologies that run through my mind as lessons.

Then my mind got transformed into the positive state that I needed for a proactive movement concerning my music: I started making phone calls to ask for directions from people who were in the music industry before me; I shot more music videos and invested in colorful clothing and props, I promoted my music with all that I had left on me; I traveled to different states to sing; I contacted my school to re-enroll for the semester and finish my thesis. I got online and sent messages to people that had supported my music in the past, and I invited them to celebrate my birthday with me by attending my concert—I organized my birthday concerts for friends and family, to listen to me as I sang praise songs on my birthday weekends at Church for two birthdays in a row of two consecutive years, while we ate food and giant cakes that were red-carpet themed; I made more jokes at home with my family even though many of my jokes might have been a bit boring but we didn't care; I called my friends to check on them— I wanted them to know that I care about them. I looked out for different opportunities to fund my music projects because music production and projects could be very expensive, but God always made a way for me. I promoted my music, while I started saving to record new songs; I was invited to have my own radio show, and I started an online radio show, where I was speaking encouraging words, and played music to my listeners until later that year when the radio station closed down; I wrote more songs based on gratitude, instead of a bitter heart.

Then the most important thing happened, and I will never forget how it changed my life beautifully—I reached out to friends who had beautiful voices and gifts in music, to encourage them to go to the studio and record their songs. I showed them the resources that I used from recording songs to album printing, and then album launch ceremony planning, and music video recording. I called to check up on them and was happy to give them information when they call me with questions about the music process. I stayed connected to my loving mentors in music, who never held back from me at any moment. I volunteered with enthusiastic friends who loved to give to the less privileged as we visited the homeless shelter. I volunteered to help the youth of a few churches, and I opened a networking opportunity to help small business owners in my city when there were none. All these occupied my mind and kept me away from depression.

As time went on, I started getting messages from people about testimonies of great things that happened to them, when they listened to my music—job offers, school admission, and answers to personal prayers. I got messages from people in countries that I had never visited. I got messages from people in other continents that I never imagined I could reach, and they told me that they watched my videos on their television from a TV station that was headquartered in Nigeria. I got phone calls from people who just wanted to send me monetary gifts even though I did not ask for any money because they said that they want to bless my music ministry.

As universal as music is, people get attracted to the life and vibrancy in your songs if they see it. Even if your songs are slow, do you bring hope to the listener? When you are shopping in the grocery store, do you smile at a random person who is looking at your nicely braided hair, your lipstick-stained tee-shirt, your chopped toenail polish, or your soil-stained flip-flops? How do you welcome the eyes that look at you? Do you give them a haughty look, or do you just look away from them? What do you tell the cashier that just checked your groceries out—do you compliment them or give them an insulting stare? The truth is that almost everyone is going through a bad day just like you, and your smile or kind words could be all they need to make it through the day; or not commit suicide after a bad 8-hour shift with their supervisor;

or not snap and say appalling words to their children at home; or to not go to the bar to get drunk and get into an accident; or to not get to a club to meet a random person that they will have a one-night sexual fling with, that would result to having a child out of their wedlock.

You may think you do not have much power, but you are more powerful than you think—and the only way that you can use that power is through your words and your actions. Your words and actions today are most likely to influence your future tomorrow, just as you are living in your present situation based on the decisions that you took in the past. If you are like me, the decisions of the past do not necessarily take us to the future that we envisioned, but there is a chance to do something today that will produce a better tomorrow.

7

SALT— The Spice of Life

I used to know someone who wanted to be the richest person in the world and would do anything to get to be one of the most powerful people on earth, even if it takes getting various degrees and certifications, and joining elite groups that can lift them to their desired dream. But I also know a few people who do not mind having a few thousand dollars, as long as they can take care of themselves and their family alone. But they do not care about the neighbor next door who may not have money to buy dinner. While some others may not run after millions, they just want to have enough to take care of their family, leave an inheritance for their children; and have extra to help other people in need.

You see, everyone has a desire to fulfill certain dreams, but our desires are often pushed by the level of discontentment or greed that we feel at certain times of our lives. It is not wrong to desire great things for our lives and set big goals for the future. You are often considered a wise person when you set positively great goals for yourself and your future. But one of the issues in setting goals is that some people do not know how to set a limit to their dreams, and these dreams start to get unrealistic or bizarre, or even evil to an extent, especially when they do not mind doing negative things to cut edges, as they pursue their goals. The biggest problem is discontentment, and greedy pursuit to find more spice for a life that has already been seasoned with salt. If only we can reduce unrealistic dreams; and replace our desires with dreams to influence the lives of other people positively, we can accomplish greater success as leaders and role models.

When I think about a life seasoned with salt. I remember this verse from the Bible:

Matthew 5:13-16 (New International Version)

"You are the salt of the earth. But if the salt loses its saltiness, how can it be made salty again? It is no longer good for anything, except to be thrown out and trampled underfoot. You are the light of the world. A town built on a hill cannot be hidden. Neither do people light a lamp and put it under a bowl. Instead, they put it on its stand, and it gives light to everyone in the house. In the same way, let your light shine before others, that they may see your good deeds and glorify your Father in heaven".

Unfortunately, we have failed to realize that we are the salt of this world, and we can bring flavor by changing the lives of people around us. We can recognize talents and potentials in people, and we help them succeed. Let me share this story with you.

Several years ago, I got an admission to pursue a graduate degree in Political Science at the University of North Texas. I was awarded funding by the department, but I had to work as a Teaching Assistant to get paid. My first assignment was to a visually impaired student, along with an additional one hundred college students in a freshman Political Science class. The other students were not as hardworking as "Beauty" (not real name), who could not see. I had to spend extra hours reading her assignments to her. She would go to bed around 2 A.M most mornings, and still get to class before 8 A.M, just to excel in her studies. I had to solicit on her behalf sometimes because the system was not considering her condition initially. However, "Beauty" did not care about what the system required. She only cared about her goals. I gave her something to work towards and promised rewards like food outings if she passed her exams. Trust me, my darling girl never disappointed me to God's Glory. She did much better than the other students who had no disability. Occasionally, she wanted to quit, but I had to encourage and pray with her. God answered, and ALL GLORY TO GOD. Eventually, I got the report that "Beauty" finished her internship successfully; and she also graduated with her bachelor's degree, which she completed in three and half years.

Here are some of the lessons that I have learned in the story above, and I want to share them as a life I hope to live:

1) God puts you in certain places to be a blessing to others. You were created to encourage someone or

some people and to help them get to the top. It is part of your ministry and destiny. There have been several times when I have wondered why I find myself at a particular place in my life, even though I did not plan to be there. Sometimes, I had a few pity parties just to force myself into depression, because I was lagging on the goals that I set for myself. But I found out that any situation or location that I find myself in at every moment of my life, is the exact place that I am destined to be, for me to fulfill a calling to success, either in my own life or in the life of someone else that would need me right then.

Your selfless service to others will be the legacy that they remember you for, not necessarily all the words that you said. If the person you are helping needs help to read and write, teach them to do so; but teach them how to teach others to do the same. In this way, you are planting a seed that tens, hundreds, thousands, or even millions of people will benefit from. Go above and beyond to help those who look up to you for guidance—sometimes it could take sleepless nights, trips to libraries, writing letters of recommendation, traveling to support games or presentations or concerts of those you mentor. Sometimes, it could cost you money, time, energy, and even random training for yourself to help the other person that you are mentoring to become better in their pursuit of success. Do it and watch how God fixes your life.

2) Never think you cannot achieve success at helping other people, because of your limitation. That is the biggest lie that you can tell yourself. When that thought comes to your mind, ask yourself: "did I help myself to eat my last meal, by lifting my food into my mouth from a plate in front of me"? If the answer is 'yes', then you can help somebody else to accomplish what they need you to guide them for. Do you have experience in what you are being asked to help them with? How were you able to accomplish success in that same situation? If you do not have the experience needed to help the person accomplish their success, do you know anybody else that you can refer them to? If you do not have a reference, can you sacrifice a little time to research on the area of expertise, for you to know how you could assist the person by directing them to the right channel for their breakthrough— while you could support them physically, financially, or even emotionally by letting them know you believe in them, and you are willing to support them in other ways they could need you as they climb the ladder to greatness? Just keep pushing till you help them get to the top—encourage people as you mentor them, with practical advice and directions that are pleasing to be emulated by others.

3) The reason you are in your position now is known to God alone, so ask God to show you what to do for His name to be glorified through your actions. Many people think they earned their position of honor as a reward for their hard work, and so they only get to the

top to enjoy the luxury it brings. But far from it, we all are called to high places to be effective by adding value to the world that we are in. This reminds me of a very scary feeling that I get when I read of Queen Esther's uncle, Mordecai's statement to her when she refused to help her fellow countrymen. She was scared for her life when the Israelites were sentenced to be killed in Persia. She tried to 'shy out' of helping them to plead to the king, even though she was a queen. She was afraid because the king did not know she was an Israelite. Her uncle made a statement that always pushes me to know that I am in a place for a reason, which is to make a positive value every time.

Esther 4:13-14 (New Living Translation)

Mordecai sent this reply to Esther: "Do not think for a moment that because you're in the palace you will escape when all other Jews are killed. If you keep quiet at a time like this, deliverance and relief for the Jews will arise from some other place, but you and your relatives will die. Who knows if perhaps you were made queen for just such a time as this?"

We should always know that if we refuse to make a positive difference in a situation that requires help, or in the life of someone that needs to excel but is struggling to make it, God will raise someone else to do it instead of us. I strive to avoid the shame of being replaced in a place where I should have performed positively to make a legendary change.

4) School can never teach you more lessons than life can teach. Do not go to school alone to learn from books. Learn from the people you meet at school and the experience you have over there too. Let school pass through you. My students

have taught me more than I learned in school, and I am not sorry to say that. I am still using most of the lessons that I learned from my encounter with them, to make some delicate decisions; to help others find their compass in life when they are stuck, and to mentor other people.

8

Microwave Generation

I am a millennial! It took me a very long time to find out that not only people born ten years after me are classified as that. Interestingly, my generation has been classified as the "Microwave Generation Y" too. I comfort myself sometimes by saying that there is a Generation Z after us, so we are not the youngest. However, I quickly admit to the fact that many people in my generation have started pursuing the 'fast life' because we want instant gratification.

We want everything fast. We do not want to cook anything that takes longer than five minutes. We do not want to stand in line to buy anything, because someone else can deliver it to us. We do not want to write our homework at school, so we just get someone to be our "tutor"; but they end up doing the whole work for us instead of teaching us, while we pay them. We don't have time to eat home-cooked meals, so we head straight to the closest fast-food drive-through. Some of us buy a lot of cereal and oatmeal in the grocery stores because we only need milk and a microwave to produce a hot breakfast with it. We can go a little extra for lunch by buying cup noodles, and we need just water and a microwave to make our satisfying noodles with it.

We do not have time to cultivate relationships, so we get on dating sites or social media in search of beautiful or handsome people to start talking to. We do not care about the future of relationships, because we did not build one on a personal and intimate level. We jump in and out of relationships at any time because there are thousands of other people who we can meet online. We do not like to talk on the phone anymore but can text a sentence since we don't have time. We do not have time to patiently clean our homes, do our laundry, or walk the dogs; so, we pay other people to do it while we browse social media.

Some of us want to be billionaires even before we graduate high school. We want to be bosses to thousands of people, even in our teenage years. We want to graduate college and get a six-figure job the next day after graduation when we walk across the stage in college. We do not want to work for anybody, but we want people to serve us. This life is not about the goals that we accomplish for our gratification, it is about the legacy that you leave behind—the lives that you touch; the destinies that you enhanced; the mouths that you fed; the careers that you molded for other people to build their wealth on; the dreams that you helped other people to fulfill positively.

Why do we have bosses who do not understand how to treat their employees—they cannot communicate effectively; they cannot train effectively; they cannot build jobs for others where the employees will love to dedicate many years in hard work to serve them? My simple answer is that it is impossible to give other people what we do not have; it is impossible to train other people on things that we have not learned. It is impossible to empathize with our employees, about things that could make them happily work for us, if we never feel the pain or need of our employees. If nobody ever mentored you, you cannot learn from the past experiences of great leaders. If you did not get sound training at school or in a vocational school or even self-teaching, you would lack the sound training of perseverance in accomplishing goals.

I remember a job that I got some years ago. My boss hired me for just two reasons: I had a little experience that was needed for the job; but he respected the fact that I could persevere to graduate from college, even though the job had nothing to do with my degree specification. He told me that he understands what it takes to sit through classes that had nothing to do with the degree that I was pursuing, just because they were compulsory university classes that I must pass, to graduate. I don't remember most of the things that I learned in many classes like college algebra or biology, but I do remember the sleepless nights; the essays and assignments; the nights I spent in the library to study for exams; and the prayers that I said in tears; the jobs I had to take as a student in my university—I was a dishwasher, I swept stairs, I cleaned bathrooms, I cooked food for people, I braided hair for others; I took out the trash every weekday on campus. These have influenced my ability to persevere through many other goals in life, even at work and in ministry.

I remember when I gained admission into secondary school, just a little before I clocked ten years old. We were mandated to recite a famous quote by Henry Wadsworth Longfellow frequently:

> "The heights by great men reached and kept were not attained by sudden flight, but they, while their companions slept, were toiling upward in the night."- **Henry Wadsworth Longfellow**.

If I were to expatiate on this quote, I think it means that we should not delay our pursuit of the accomplishments that we dream of, as sluggards do. We do not need to take a nap to think about something that we could solve immediately; we do not need to spend hours asleep lazily if we have a goal to meet. In my observation of great people, they get to work hard even at night when others are sleeping. I used to work for a very wealthy man, but I noticed that he worked late at night, but was the first to get to work at 7 AM the next morning, before others who resume at 9 AM. No wonder he had more than three businesses and was a multimillionaire but was able to keep his wealth because he spent his time studying different areas of the economy— for his investment opportunities to expand. There was no time I went into his office, that I do not see a couple of new books about real estate, or law, or oil and gas. He tries to increase his knowledge so that he will be able to handle his business in alignment of the economical and technological trends in that industry. Most times when I mention new business opportunities to him, he already knows the lucrative options and the not-too-profitable ones. If he does not know much about it, he goes to study about it first and then gets back to me with his decision later. I noticed this lifestyle of his, and I adopted it because I saw how my knowledge of subject matters, technology, law, international news, and spirituality could influence the decisions that I make in my daily life. If you are not knowledgeable about a certain business, you do not have to go into that business because many people are doing it. It is okay to read about that business, or even take courses on that business for you to be capable of handling it. It is easier to get rich than to keep the riches that you have acquired. There are some extra-curricular activities that we do not have to engage in if it does not benefit our goals. There are some parties that we do not have to attend if we are not going to gain any profit from spending our precious time with the people that will be attending the party. Please do not get me wrong, there is nothing wrong with extra-curricular activities or parties, but not all of them are beneficial to us when we have more valuable things to do with our time. If you know that you are only attending a party because you want other people to see your beautiful dress, you honestly must evaluate if your attendance will be useful to you, except if you are going to advertise that dress for people to buy from you at that party. If the reason was for the latter, then you will gain your precious time with a profit of selling the modeled dress at the party; but you would be wasting your time if you only went to the party to show off your dress.

The quote by Henry Wadsworth Longfellow was the guideline of our school, and we were trained to toil for our high school degree in a semi-military way. I attended an Air Force secondary school, where we were trained strictly to adapt to any situation that we find ourselves, and not to rely on luxury. It was a boarding school for all students, and you had to start from the first year at the school. Nobody was allowed to join as a student at any time in the middle of the six-year secondary school program—if you do not start as a first-year student, then you could not be admitted into the school. I remember that we were not allowed to use deodorants, so we had to apply powder under our armpits, to avoid body odor.

Just like every other female in the school, I had to shave my head for the first three years as a Junior Secondary School student but was allowed by the school in the fourth year as a Senior Secondary Student to start growing my hair back. Even though I was given the freedom to grow my hair, we still had to comply with the rules for the weekly mandated hairstyles that our head female prefect gave us each Friday. We were not allowed to bring candies, cookies, cereal, drinks, or any food at all. We were only allowed to eat what was given to us at the dining hall, and we had to be smart to eat our food. The reason I said so was that we were assigned tables per fourteen people each. The boys used to play games to embezzle the food that was given to the table so that they will all eat it and leave the girls hungry till the next meal—this act was named 'smashing'. Then, the girls would revenge by "smashing" the food for the next meal or the next day, to pay back the boys for their actions.

We lived for six years in the boarding school, and only went home during mid-term break, and then the end-of-term holiday. Our families and friends were allowed to visit us once a month, but the rules were changed at some point and the visiting days were decreased. I remember that there was a time when our family was only allowed to visit us once in three months, before our holidays at end of term. Our best days were the "visiting days" when our parents came to visit us at school, and they brought us food from home, along with many snacks which we were not allowed to take back to the hostel with us to finish, except if we smuggled it to munch for the following few days. Of course, there were no mobile phones to call our family, and nor was there internet for social media. Our school was in the middle of two states, and so it was in the jungle. There were no houses or buildings around it, and the only thing you see at the gate is a "guardroom" that was always occupied by military personnel. There was no way to escape that jungle because the road outside that gate is a highway for travelers going to the next state.

One of the greatest lessons that I will never forget is the implication of stealing. This fateful occurrence happened during our second term in one of my junior high school years. The second term of every school year in Nigeria is from January to April. Those months are notoriously known for water scarcity, which is very challenging for boarding school students in a jungle like ours. Since we drink only water from the borehole or the water that we draw out from the well, there is more probability to spend a lot of time at the well on water scarcity days. This is because the senior students would send the junior students like me to fetch many buckets of water for them, and I must make sure that their buckets are filled to the brim for them to take their shower with some of it, and drink the remaining before I can fetch my own water. Sometimes, a senior student can take the chance to bully their juniors for the buckets of water, and the junior has no choice but to go back to the well for more water to refill. This could last several hours in the day, so the junior gets so tired and hungry. But the junior must still wash, dry, and iron the senior student's clothes before bed. Keep in mind that the junior still has to study for his or her personal class, also do homework, and did I mention I would still have to do my laundry too? Sometimes, it gets so tedious for the junior that it takes sleepless nights to excel in schoolwork.

I was so tired on one of those days, and I had no water to drink at night. There was no more water from the borehole, and I could not go to draw water from the well because the dormitory gate was closed. I was thirsty, hungry, and tired from all that stressful runaround for the day. So, I resorted to the laundry room, where most senior students put their buckets of water. It was dark anyway, and I knew nobody would see me do it. It was something that the "cunny students" used to do, but I never had to do it in the past because I spent more time fetching water for seniors and myself. I thought to myself "this is a school where survival is to the fittest, I better do what other people do to avoid thirst before going to bed." On this dramatic day, I took out some water from a random bucket, and I took a sip. Unfortunately, the random bucket contained a soaked cloth in bleach and detergent. I instantly spat it out and immediately headed to bed with regretful tears. I did not bother going back to take water from another bucket anymore, because this lesson was "once bitten, twice shy" for me.

I can laugh today at this experience, but it has taught me a few lessons as I grew up. The first thing is not to get in the crowd to do what other people are doing. If you do not get caught, you will suffer the repercussions on your own—either financially, health-wise, spiritually, or even in marriage. The second lesson is to work harder for what I eat and drink, instead of trying to secretly steal it from someone else. Perhaps, if I had set a cup of water for myself as I fetched water for others, I would not have to steal or "fap" from others—as we say the slang for stealing in my school is "fap".

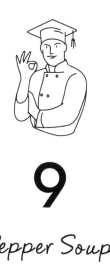

9

Pepper Soup

I used to cook food as an undergraduate student several years ago, and one of the dishes that my customers bought from me was the Pepper Soup dish, with options of goat meat or fish; served with white rice. I loved cooking the pepper soup because many people believe the hot spice helps them heal from allergies or sinus infections. Some people like to eat it during the cold season, while others love to eat the dish with their friends, as they drink and make merry. The dish is very fast to cook, and it is easy to season, as long as you performed your due diligence in seasoning your meat or fish while you boiled it in water from the beginning. The habanero pepper should also be boiled in the water from scratch so that it marinates as the meat or fish boils with salt, bouillon cubes, and onions to make it soft and give a savory aroma. Though I grind the habanero with garlic and ginger in a food processor first, before boiling the mixture in water—different people have their styles of cooking the dish. Once the meat or fish is boiled, you can add some more water, and your other ingredients like ginger, garlic, mint, more dry pepper, and bay. Some people add thyme for more flavor, but it depends on the person cooking. Bring the soup to boil and turn off your cooker when you see that the condiments and the meat or fish are perfectly cooked. Your hot and spicy dish is ready. You can eat it with yam, potatoes, bread, plantain, or rice. Though it is very spicy, you could find yourself asking for more after the first round, because of the flavorful taste of the soup.

Pepper soup reminds me of life in general, with people that love to underestimate, belittle, or hate others—they are the ones that are called 'haters' in the 21st-century language. Some people just want to tarnish your hard work, to delay you from getting to the peak of success before them. Life could be seen in some ways as pepper soup. Though it is the pepper for some, it is spicy and delicious for others. There is a slang in my country of origin that I laugh at when people say it. The slang is 'pepper them, which really means 'make them feel regrets for what they did', or 'make them feel remorseful', or 'make them jealous to the extent that they get depressed'. We call them the 'pepper dem gang'. As humans, there are so many reasons why we love to make our haters or enemies feel remorseful or regretful because they are not in our clique, or because they underestimated us in the past. There are many reasons why we do not have to make our enemies feel remorseful especially if we have nothing to show up or boast about. Some parents want their children to excel so that their friends will see them as more successful. They do not care about how many enemies they make based on their actions, but all they want to see is that they are at the top of the table and nobody else can do better than them. Meanwhile, some people just want to show off their accomplishments because they have been underestimated to an extent that it is almost unbelievable to see them successful. Those kinds of people are willing to show others the way to success but are also very quick to refer to the hassle they had to endeavor in their pasts amid the societal odds that were against them, and the journey they had to take to get to the top. Regardless of the reasons why we like to pepper our enemies or 'haters', we see reasons why we do not want to remain underestimated for a long time, either because of depression or just the fear of not fitting in. Sometimes even some of our teachers and professors who put their trust in us are the driving force to our accomplishments so that they could showcase us as products of success in their careers as educationists and academicians. Sometimes it is our friends, who want to show us that they believe in us and that they do not want others to see us as failures because we are their friends. Regardless of what it is, there is always a positive and negative effect of playing a role in the "pepper dem gang"—you only win if you had good motives to show success, despite the trials and tribulations that you had to go through. If your story tells of a breakthrough even against all odds, you are an example of the positive lesson that "pepper dem" teaches. However, if you just want to play a "pepper dem" on people who did not do any harm to you in the past, you are only wasting your time and acquiring enemies unnecessarily.

I remember an incident that happened some years ago. I got admitted into a graduate program a few weeks after I graduated with my bachelor's degree, and I was excited. The reason why I wanted this was that I started an undergraduate research fellowship at my school, where I researched the effect of judicial independence in Africa. I was privileged to attend a conference in Chicago, to present this research; and I also got the big opportunity to present the same research on Scholars Day at my college. It was a great privilege to see my mother and her friends attending the talk, and they had the opportunity to contribute to the discussion with my professors, after my presentation. Because of the progress I foresaw in my undergraduate research fellowship, I decided to pursue a graduate degree too, so that I could find more interesting things about judicial independence in Africa—I wanted to learn about this because it was a practical subject that was not explored about Africa, and I knew that I could use the resources in the United States educational system to find more data for Africa and the whole world too. This could be a solution for consultants of transitioning governments in the future, but I had to do something about solving this piece of the puzzle. So, I chose to study comparative politics on a higher level.

A few years later, in the graduate program at my school, I had to represent my school at a different conference organized by Political scholars in another state, where I presented my research paper. At that time, I was working on a quantitative analysis research which was based on restorative justice and judicial independence in Africa, with my professor. This subject meant a lot to me because I was inspired by my professor who happened to be my committee chair. I felt it was a golden opportunity for me to be working on a topic that had not been treated with enough esteem in Africa, and there was no quantitative analysis that could prove the measure of an independent judiciary in the African system—regarding restorative justice. In simple terms, this really meant that there was no quantitative analysis in the world that was measuring the effects of restorative justice on judicial independence in the continent of Africa, and my research would have been the first quantitative analysis in the whole continent to do so. That was my dream, I wanted to be a pacesetter in the continent of Africa for something, as a young woman and an immigrant into the United States.

I was excited, and I spent so much time researching with my professor on different articles and research that had been published on restorative justice in Africa in the past. So, I worked on the literature review of my paper that I was going to present at the conference, and my professor who was going to collaborate with me on this research worked on the quantitative measure analysis of the research. However, I had cited another professor who did very good work on the articles for restorative justice in Africa but did not have the quantitative analysis on it yet. As fate would have it, that professor was the discussant for the panel at the conference where I was presenting the research paper.

I started with the presentation of my literature review, and I mentioned that I cited this scholar along with many other scholars in the research article, but I also noted that their work did not have the quantitative analysis that could prove the effect of judicial independence and restorative justice. I did not see anything negative in what I said, I only mentioned the lack of quantitative analysis as a piece of the puzzle that I was willing to solve. I was taught in graduate school that your academic research should always leave a space for others to keep working on your previous work so that the perfect results could be found in the future. You may not find the perfect solution, but your work could be a foundation for others to build on. As previously planned for our collaborative presentation, my co-author who happened to be my professor in college, took over the presentation and showed the quantitative analysis for the research; he also demonstrated our findings.

To my surprise, the professor who was one of the many scholars that I cited, and who happened to be the discussant lashed me badly when it was time to give feedback on my research presentation at the conference, even in the presence of many professors and prestigious people. This discussant told me with so much wrath in their voice, that I did not do my research well and I was not experienced enough to know that they had the quantitative work. Since the discussant could not face my co-author who happens to be the most published in his field, the discussant's safest way to tackle my co-author and me, was to vent their anger on me, because I was just a graduate student. We all knew that the discussant was agitated because nobody had ever pointed out any discrepancy in their work, since this discussant was one of the pacesetters who started research on African judiciary, talk less of a small first-year graduate student that I was. Our dear discussant refused to see the positive solution that we have found to complete the beautiful work that their own published work had started.

When we returned to Denton from the conference, my professor called me into his office and asked me how I felt about the discussant's comments at the conference. I told him I did not care about what the discussant said, because I know that we did great at that conference, and we introduced something that many people have not been able to find. My professor is a gifted man who realizes that nothing comes easy in life, and many people will try to make it worse for you if you let them. So, he sat me down to tell me a story. He said:

> "Look, in my first year in Graduate School, I went to a conference just like you to present my research. The discussant at that panel lambasted me so much that I ran out of the room after my presentation, and I puked. I had never vomited like that in my life. I felt dejected, I felt that I was dumb and did not know anything. However, I was determined to make a great name and success in all that I do, which you see today in my career. Today I can tell you that the same discussant was involved in a scandal and lost his job, and he's nowhere to be found because he did not end well as a professor. But you know and see how far I have come in my career, and how much I have made with being a highly successful political scientist and academician. I have published a lot of political research in comparative politics all over the world. Listen to my advice, do not let anybody put you down, they are not worth it. Keep your head up high and watch how great you will be, and how far you will go in the future."

That talk with my professor was the best day of my life as a graduate student, and I will never trade that experience for anything else. I walked out of his office with the highest confidence that I had ever felt. I was determined to be like my professor, and I looked up to him as a mentor till I graduated. I am thankful that he saw a gift in me, and he built me to produce greatness with it.

Some years later in 2014, my professor submitted my research for publication in a scholarly journal, and that was the beginning of me seeing the light in political research. In 2016, our research was published for the world to see by a journal of African and Asian studies— and scholars in biology, law, and political scientists started to cite our work. That right there was one of my greatest experiences of the 'pepper dem gang'. I interpreted it as a push for me to strive and work hard to accomplish my greatest dream of being the first person to publish a quantitative analysis on the effects of restorative justice on judicial independence in Africa, even though it was very hard to find data. My professor always told me to ignore what anybody else said about me so that I could go higher. He told me to prove myself, so that I would not point accusing fingers, without giving a solution to problems that nobody had ever solved. He told me to watch and see myself win. And guess what? I am still watching and win-ING. That is one of the prices that you must pay as a pacesetter, not only to just make haters very jealous or dejected but to put a solution to the world that nobody else knows—so that you can help people that need direction. I know that many people have read the article, and I was so excited one day when I saw that a law school in Canada uses my research in their classroom for one of their compulsory reading assignments in their academic year.

Who would think that this young inexperienced African girl can make a little difference for others to see and work on? Isn't that life? Where people think that you can never accomplish what you have dreamt of because they are much better than you; and where people think that they can pull you down with all their power and strength and wrath because you are flying and excelling above them. My question to you today is: would you allow them to pull you down, or would you rise and aim for the sky? Would you work hard even when everything else seems to be working against you when colleagues think that you are not good enough to do the things that the world would accept? Would you look away from all the disadvantages and the cons that are against you, and face all the pros in your life as a selling point for your greatness? Or would you stay silent and put your head down instead of raising it high, and walking with your shoulders high to show the world that you have got some talents and values that nobody else has?

Sometimes, we are our own worst critics—we feel so less competent in the things that God has given us to use for his glory. That is why a lot of people have so many challenges that they hold back instead of using or even trying to improve on their talents because they think they are not as good as who they see on TV or who they hear every day on the radio or online. Who told you that you are not as good as that person? Do you know how long it took that person to be able to stand in front of the crowd to sing, speak, act, or do everything that you see them do? It is the best choice for every human to build upon the things that they know they can do with their strength, passion, and will.

I will use myself as the perfect example again because I am writing this book and it is easy for me to make my life experiences as the case study. I used to think I was not good enough to sing in front of people because people did not appreciate my coarse-textured alto voice in the beginning when I joined the choir. I used to just sing as a background singer, and those with the lovely soprano voices would take the lead. It did not bother me as much because I just loved to sing, until one day when a minister noticed that I was singing a song at rehearsals and closing my eyes with so much passion. He walked up to the music director and asked the music director to tell me to stand up and sing this song at the rehearsal, and the music director agreed. The minister then said to the music director, "I want her to sing the song because she has so much passion for that song that I think she is the best person that would sing it tomorrow morning." I sang the song the next morning, which was a Sunday service, and I never stopped singing at that church nor any other church since that day— just because someone saw me and believed I could do it. I sang on that Sunday, and the whole Church was so revived to the Glory of God.

My music director saw how the audience welcomed my voice and assigned me to lead worship songs almost every week. Soon after, I sang a song that became almost the anthem of our services. This is because my Pastor loved the song so much, and we sang it almost every week for two years. We would even go to different events as a choir, and I would be asked to sing the song. Being in the choir groomed me to lead the crowd in different songs, and I felt happy that my passion did not die. One day, my church had to go for a zonal program, and the choir had to merge with other churches' choirs too. I was asked to lead in praise songs, which I did with so much joy. When I finished, I went back to my seat without thinking anything would happen further. To my surprise, however, three Caucasian men who sat next to me gave me a note that I will never forget. All it said was:

> "For the gifts and the calling of God are irrevocable." Romans 11:29 (English Standard Version)

They were missionaries who came to share the Bible from Gideon ministries. They had arrived at the event while I was singing, and they saw how everyone was dancing and praising God. They saw the manifestation of God's Spirit on the praise and had to write that note to me even though they did not know me. I collected the paper from one of them, and I read the note. I was stunned! How can God give me something that he will not collect back from me? Does he love me so much that he could use the gift, but never take it away? I was happy to get a confirmation that my singing is not just a passionate hobby, it is a gift that my heavenly father gave me to use for the world to feel his love. That night, I decided to use that irrevocable gift as extremely as possible; with every dime and energy that I could get. I must confess that I fall short of this determination sometimes, but I am grateful that God never falls short of His promise.

What is that talent you must spend your time on today? What have you heard about the gifts that you have? Do you know that your gifts are the only things in life that can change other people's lives and destinies? Do you know that your gifts will make an easy way for you if you just keep pressing on with them? Though it may take some time, you just need to keep pushing, training, improving, planning, working hard, building, learning, producing fruits from it—and your story will change for good one day. Keep praying and hoping as you work hard to get to the top.

I am grateful that I was born into a family of performing arts, so my love for music was inbuilt. I was born in Nigeria, to the late Col. David Bankole Laoye (Rtd), who was the acting state administrator/military governor of the Old Western State in Nigeria; and my mother is Temitayo Taiwo, an international performing artiste. I attribute a big part of my talent to my mother's gift. I was motivated to be in the performing arts because I was proud to see pictures of my mother acting for President Regan at the Smithsonian American Art Museum in 1980, where the president gave her and seven other artists a diplomatic brooch. My mother had been selected to travel with the ex-President Shehu Shagari during his regime as the Nigerian President, because she was Prof. Wole Soyinka's lead actress "Sidi", in the play titled "Lion and the Jewel". At a young age, I was motivated to use my talents in singing and writing, when I saw pictures of my mother's Broadway performance and many other creative artworks in her art gallery. Also, I believe that I inherited some performing artistic skills from my paternal grandfather—Though he was an educated pharmacist who had a kingdom to rule, the late king of Ede, Oba John Adetoyese Laoye continued to play the talking drum, and pulled international attraction to the Nigerian talking drums, with his passion for showcasing the African culture. He was known for playing the talking drums for Queen Elizabeth on her visit.

So how did I get into music professionally? I kept singing in the choir and sometimes went to sing at other churches. But I did not go directly into recording songs, until after I graduated with my bachelor's degree, and returned to the same college for my graduate school. On the first week that I got to my new apartment, as I unpacked to prepare for the next phase of my life as a graduate student, I realized that I would not be accomplishing anything tangible in life if I did not pursue my irrevocable passion of music. I felt there was a missing part of me, that a graduate degree could not fill— it was music. While I was a graduate student, I was given funding by the department at my school and was assigned a job as a graduate teaching assistant— I had to assist the professors of two different political science classes. One of my undergraduate students in the political science class was a young Nigerian man, who later joined my church after the semester that he took my class. He started playing the guitar in my church choir and pointed out that there is a music studio on campus, which is free for all our university students because it is a charge that was already included in our tuition as a school amenity. So, I asked him to go to my college music studio with me for a freestyle to a song in mind. He played the guitar, while I sang the lead, the alto, and soprano background voices for that song. That first visit to the studio gave me an experience of studio recording. I got the song from the studio engineer, and I released it online.

I contacted people to mentor me. I sent emails to great people that were songwriters, producers, recording artists, and entertainers. I got a response from most of them and got on the phone. I knew I needed help in gaining experience in the music business, and I sent a message to two twin brothers, who did one of the biggest favors anybody could do for a stranger. They agreed to mentor me. One of them trained my voice every week; while his brother wrote a song for me to sing with him for free. I contacted a friend of mine in Nigeria, who is a prestigious music producer and I told him of my plans to travel to Nigeria for my best friend's wedding around Christmas 2013, and about my desire to record a few songs. He encouraged me to come over to his studio and told me how much he would charge me. I was just a graduate student with little money, but I withdrew all that I had in my bank account; and I went to Nigeria for three weeks, during my winter break. That was how I recorded my first album in January 2014.

I came back to the United States after recording, but I did not have the money to print out CDs or shoot any music videos. However, I held onto the songs and played them for my friends, hoping that one day I will find someone to help me with the money to complete my project. I continued going to school, but I decided to do some more things like taking professional pictures for my album art, and I decided to release one of the songs in a slideshow video on YouTube. Of course, this decision was made after I prayed about finding someone that could help me financially to complete this music project. I shared the song on Facebook, and I sent it to many people via direct messages on Facebook as well.

To my surprise, a kind man of God heard this song and asked me what I needed to release the album that I was working on. I told him the amount, and he asked me to travel down to see him in Houston where he was having a Christian crusade. I boarded a bus to Houston, and I met him over there with the last penny that I had on me. He greeted me warmly at the crusade in Houston, and he asked me to go back to Dallas but promised to speak with me later in the week. I was a bit skeptical because I did not know if he would fulfill his promise. Again, to my surprise, he called me a few days later to let me know that he had sent me the money I needed to finish my album printing; build a website, and create business materials like cards and flyers. That was how I was able to complete my first music album, which I have been able to independently sell over 3,000 copies of it in five years— this may look small to you, but you may not understand how challenging it is to sell CDs to over 3,000 strangers who are not your friends or family— the majority of them did not speak my native language, neither were they from my country. I have also been able to shoot five music videos in seven years, and I am grateful for great testimonies from people to God's glory. Though I am working on other songs now with a Yamaha Ambassador, and I have shot another video from my second biggest music project so far. I am happy that I took that leap of faith in the first instance.

What is it that you must do to accomplish that dream that you have been holding for years? Why not do it today, by going on your knees in prayers and asking God to direct you in the way that he knows will take you to your destiny? He always answers prayers, and he answers prayers in ways that we do not even expect. Sometimes we have to wait for him to do his work for a little longer than we wish, but sometimes he is quick to answer, and we always get good results from the prayers that we take before him—it may be just what we wanted, or better than we asked for, but it may also be a prayer that He answers at a later time which would be a better option to what we wanted in the first place.

10

"It's All Beans"

Yesterday was Valentine's Day, and I had beans. I gave away the chocolates and whatever the day had to offer, for a palatable plate of beans—I mean the Nigerian honey beans, cooked with tomatoes, peppers, onions, oil, and crayfish. You cannot go wrong with the aroma of that crayfish in your beans, and the spice melting with soft beans in your mouth. I had mine with bread, and it felt like a million-dollar plate. I never used to like beans as a child, and I was often tricked to eat them only when I hear the deceptive warning that 'only beans can make you tall, so you must eat them to grow tall.' I innocently ate beans with the hope of growing tall as a young girl; but why is it that after almost 30 years of that myth, my five foot and 6 inches body has not grown taller than an average person who is my age? The answer is simple—it is just beans! It is an untrue myth that nobody needs to tell anymore, except you are just trying to get a child to eat the beans that you painstakingly cooked for three hours. Looking back at that time when the myth seemed true, and my ferocious bean-eating habit in a desperate quest to grow tall, I have concluded that the lie of height increase is 'just beans'. In Nigeria, when we hear a myth that people are fast to believe even to the detriment of their health or wellness, we say "all na beans"—meaning all the lies and myths are just untrue imaginations and fables that are used by people to deceive others, usually for the story-teller's gain or advantage. Unfortunately, people grow with the mindset of these stories and rumors, that it sometimes affects the rest of their lives, even to the point of passing on the fables to future generations.

An example of the "just beans" stories that a lot of young Nigerian women were told in the past was that they should not obtain too many degrees before marriage, because no man wants to marry a successful woman. But many women got to realize after they grew up that many men do not mind marrying women that have achieved a lot of good things like bagging multiple degrees before marriage. In fact, many men are attracted to marrying women with engineering, law, medical, theology, architectural, and even doctoral degrees in this 21st century. My mom used to tell me when I was young that: "if a man loves you, he will be proud of you." Not all men are egoistic and domineering, some men want the best for their wives just as they want for themselves too. They believe a successful couple can influence their children and the whole society by showing accomplishments and attributes to emulate.

At every stage in our life, there are two types of people that I personally believe have been designed to stay with us at that moment: some are the naysayers— that cause us to work hard to prove them wrong. I call them the cause of 'motivation' because their wrong judgment about us and their negative predictions are the reasons why we are motivated to strive for success. The second type of people are mostly friends and family, or other loved ones that believe in our work, talents, skills, brains, and decisions. They are the people who will not stop supporting us every step of the way, even against all odds and obstacles that try to stop us. They do not mind traveling overseas or climbing mountains for you, and they keep encouraging you to focus and persevere through the pains or delays because they believe in brighter light at the end of the tunnel for you. Those are my favorite types of people that I always want to keep close to myself, and I call them by the standard that they use to keep me going, 'team endurance'. They are the 'real deal, and they will not stop being your fan until kingdom comes. They have seen you shed blood and tears; they have witnessed doors closing on you in business and relationships, and they have seen you fall once and have picked you up seven times. It is from the voices of these that I hear the Voice of God— because they remind me that only He has a purpose for my life. They remind me that he gave me every natural endowment for His Glory to shine forever in me so that the world can see His love through me.

There are times when I have cried and complained about my calling in ministry, especially when God gives me an assignment that I do not think that I can do well. I set limitations for myself, based on the lies that other people have told me in the past. They have made judgments of me even when I was suffering from an illness, which caused me to bleed for years. How downcast could a person who spent multiple routines for Doctor's appointments per week feel, when they finally see someone that they loved mocking them by saying, "you are growing too fat. Go and lose weight. You do not look as beautiful as you used to be". Or how about another statement from a loving boyfriend, who was so in love with me a few months before an illness but got so discouraged and said "I am sorry, I cannot be with you anymore because I cannot deal with all these things you are going through. The weight gain, the bleeding, the pains are all too much for me to stay." Well, at least he apologized for that sad experience eight years later, after he saw a someone else suffering from the same illness. I guess some people have to experience a situation that they blindly judge so that they can understand the pain of those who they criticize. There is another one, how would it feel if an insensitive friend tells you, "That guy that came to shake your hand likes you, and he is my very good friend. But when I spoke with him, we think that you are too fat." That appalling statement was from a "friend" who was probably wearing a size 18 or 20 in U.S sizes, when I was wearing a size 10 dress, and size 12. I looked right back at her to give an immediate response to her statement and told her "You just described yourself. Go and look in the mirror." How about a statement that I heard from a friend of mine in another city, whose classmates said she was not smart enough, but the instructors were only giving her and other students good grades, in partiality. Oh well, where were they when she spent all night studying in the library? When she did not sleep in two days, or even took only a couple of hours' nap in three days. Were they there at 2 A.M, when she almost pulled out her hair to study econometrics, or to read hundreds of research journal articles for a peer review assignment that she had to write?

Here is how we think of such people: how do you even sleep at night, knowing that your hurtful rumors hurt other people? I guess you are so immune to positive emotions, since your youth; and you were treated to hate other people and bring them down for you to feel good. Unfortunately, your feeling is only temporary because your evil minds always keep those who carry them like you sleepless, hateful, and restless.

When you realize that your enemies are weak, you should torment them with your success. Never let someone else pull you down because of their own inferiority complex, which has developed into a mental problem for them. If you know that you are in the image of your creator, and you possess all attributes that He has, then ride on to success by strategically building an innovation that will change the world. Do something different from the trend of the world and find solutions to the problems around you. Every human being has a calling from God, and your calling is a solution to problems that nobody else can solve better than you. When you realize this, you do not need to respond to naysayers with your words, you only need to work harder to produce your shining gift to their astonishment. It always works perfectly!

On those times when I am in the pity-party mood that I described above, I always remember this scripture that opposes the limitations I had set for myself. When the Lord told me to author this book for publication, I was excited over ten years ago. However, when the Spirit of God told me that I should write this book in a way that the reader would learn some lessons from my past experience, I was hesitant. I gave so many excuses for why I am not good enough to write this book because my classmate told me I was a sloppy writer many years ago— but I failed to remember that my boss told me some years later, that he was happy to read my legal requests in auditing over a million dollars for our global company. He was so impressed by the documentation, that he had to forward the email to everybody on the team. This was not a small company; it is one of the largest global companies in the world—with thousands of branches in almost all countries on earth. Well, maybe my writing improved in all these years as I grew older with more experience, but I still always had a mental reminder of that spiteful classmate's public comment as I stood in front of the whole class and watched as everybody gasped at his comments to me. I forgot that this same classmate was the originator of a rumor against some students in the past, and such people that have natural hateful characters will always reflect their real personalities in their speech. The only thing you can do to these people is to show them, love, through your actions. There is no need to respond to them verbally with spiteful words— instead, thank them for their comment, and use some of the criticism as constructive feedback to improve on yourself. Let this motivate you to learn better and grow in the skills that you already have. I realized that the spiteful feedback from people like this young man was one of the limitations that I subjected my mind to believe for many years, with the fear of being rejected in the future. Then God led me to this scripture:

Exodus 4:11-12 (New International Version

11 The Lord said to him, "Who gave human beings their mouths? Who makes them deaf or mute? Who gives them sight or makes them blind? Is it not I, the Lord?

12 Now go; I will help you speak and will teach
you what to say."

This book is the product of a limitation that I previously
set for myself, but I have now broken through it for the world
to see.

11

Birthright for a Plate of Red Porridge

think I would introduce more people to the Nigerian yam porridge. Not only is it delicious, but it also fills you up so easily because of the yam—the heavy carbs could put you to bed if you are too full after eating. It is cooked with diced boiled yams, fried with palm oil in a stew of tomatoes, peppers, onions, crayfish, and seasonings. Some people include chopped meats or dried stockfish for more volume in the recipe. Honestly, when I remember the story of how Esau sold his birthright because of a plate of porridge in the Bible, I am tempted to think that the porridge in the Bible might have been like the Nigerian red porridge.

So many times, we tend to give up some valuable things for other less-profitable ones because we are impatient to ignore the few minutes of pleasure. In a real sense, some of us have gotten into relationships that offered only short-time pleasures, even though we knew it was not going to be worth it. Some of us have quit our life-fulfilling jobs and ministry because we wanted to pursue a career that would pay us more salaries for just a few months or two years. Some of us have turned down a marriage proposal from a young man, who was hardworking with prospects of a successful future, just because we wanted to be with a hip-hop artist who had been signed to a three-year record label deal. We do not care if the hip-hop star will not be rich after their three years of stardom. We do not even try to ask if he has plans that will establish him after his stardom expires, like educational or vocational training; or even investments to secure a good financial future. We just want the pleasures now, and we can trade better options that had long-term results. Do not get me wrong, I am not saying hip-hop artists do not have money after their contracts are over with record labels. This is just a statement for us all to be considerate of our future, even as we enjoy the present times.

Some of us need to train our children not to get carried away with the immediate gratification of food they get from anywhere, especially in this present time. Here is a story that I would like to share:

When I was eight years old, there was a day that God showed me His extreme love and protection, through an inhumane experience that was prevented by my mother. I was playing downstairs alone in my grandfather's house, and a very close employee/accomplice of the family came to deliver some reports to my grandparents since he was an employee of my grandfather. This man was in charge of my grandfather's agricultural estate, including some of the businesses associated with it. As he finished eating with my family upstairs, he met me playing alone downstairs and offered me a brown-colored butter mint candy. He was smiling and watched me as I jumped gallantly to show my mother the sweet. He thought I would lick the candy without showing my mom. Immediately my mother saw the sweet, she flushed it in the toilet. I cried my eyes out, but I knew I would get many more sweets and biscuits from my mom. Many years later, I realized that it was a blessing to show my mother that little sweet. The sweet which was supposed to be cream-colored, as the regular butter mint candy in Nigeria should be, was brown colored. It was poisoned by that man, who had wrapped the candy in the blood that was infected with HIV/AIDS. He confessed many years afterward, that he had done the same thing to some other children. Please teach your children to show you everything they receive from everyone, not just strangers. It is very important to their lives. Thanks to my mother for teaching me life-saving values, and I give God all the Glory for parents who care for us in love.

The biggest thing that causes us to desire instant gratification at the expense of the most valuable things in our lives, is greed. Only greed will make you accept something that is against your morals.

Here is another story of three people, that I would love to share as a lesson on "not selling your birthright for a plate of porridge." It is a story of a man in a Nigerian University, who was dating two girlfriends. He liked them both and was quite confused about which one to pick. The first girlfriend was so lively, and she loved to be the life of every party. She was beautiful, and quite a diva that was nicknamed "Ms. Fun-lover. She was very smart and gave generously because she was from a very wealthy home. She had an amazing attitude, and everybody liked her a lot. She never had any records of arguments, jealousy, envy, gossip, or racism. As jovial as she was, she was mindful of her speech and never said hurtful words to people. She was courteous and respected everybody equally—she gave the same regard to both prestigious people, and the less privileged too. You would love her if you ever got to meet her. The second girlfriend was a bit reserved and conservative in character. She was a good cook, and everyone liked to visit her because she always had food to give her guests on campus. She was equally brilliant, and spent more time studying in the library, or visiting her boyfriend. Compared to the other girlfriend, she was not born with a silver spoon. She was a recipient of the national scholarship, which sponsored all her tuition, housing, and feeding allowance too. She loved her boyfriend more because he was the only person that she felt comfortable sharing delicate topics and secrets with. Even though people liked to visit her because she liked cooking and they also loved to eat her food too, she was not close to a lot of them except her boyfriend. The boyfriend was not from a wealthy home but was not from a poor home either. He came from a middle-class family, who could easily afford the necessities in the home—including sound education in good schools, quality clothing, and good food.

After a few years, the three of them graduated with their bachelor's degrees. The first girlfriend got admitted into a University in California, for her master's degree; while the second girlfriend got an entry-level job as a secretary at a small business because she planned to save the money that she made from her salary to use for enrolling in graduate school. The man gained admission to two different Universities in

Nigeria for his doctoral degree, which were proposing full funding to pay his school fees and housing. While this was going on, the boyfriend impregnated the lady who was from a less privileged home but did not tell the rich girlfriend.

One day, the rich girlfriend notified her boyfriend that she was going to the United States for her master's degree, and her father was offering him a full sponsorship to travel with her too—however, he had to agree to a condition of marrying the rich girl before they travel. The boyfriend agreed and got married to the rich girlfriend. He stopped all communication with the other girlfriend that he impregnated, and he moved to the United States with the rich lady that he married. He declined both admissions that he was offered for a doctoral degree in Nigeria because he was hoping to study abroad after relocation. The pregnant girlfriend found out about the wedding and relocation of her boyfriend, after a little while. She was disowned by her parents because of the pregnancy and was left alone to take care of her baby. She suffered from the trauma of being duped during the pregnancy, but she encouraged herself, and she gave birth to twins. After the birth of her babies, she quit her job, to startup a small fashion design business that would allow her to nurse her children, while she used the profit of the small business for feeding herself and the children. She started the business because she could not afford a babysitter, and the children were very little. She struggled to feed the children and endured hungry nights on so many occasions. She lived in a slum area of Lagos because that was all she could afford; she started homeschooling her children a few months before their third birthday because she could not afford kindergarten for them. The children continued to grow in stature, wisdom, and strength despite the hardship in their family till their fifth birthday. However, she continuously strived to promote her business, and she shared pictures of some of the beautiful clothes that she had made on social media.

One day, a very prominent wife of a politician saw one of her dresses on Instagram, and she contacted the fashion designer. She mentioned that she was traveling to Ethiopia, for a conference held for African women in power, which also included wives of presidents and politicians. She ordered ten outfits for her trip because she believed that her fashion would make a perfect statement at the conference. The fashion designer was grateful for the opportunity and made highly creative dresses as ordered. She was paid handsomely for her great work, and she used the money to enroll her children in a decent school; rent a better apartment in a safer area; and open a boutique, where she sold the clothes that she made in addition to the custom-made orders that she was known for. Her breakthrough came when the politician's wife called her again. This time, she was calling from Ethiopia with seven other women from different African countries, who wanted the same dresses she had made. In addition, one of the women was the wife of the president of an African country, and she requested to speak with her concerning a consulting job. She was planning a program in her country, to train widows to learn different trades including fashion design. The program already hired trainers in that country, but it would be more useful and interesting if the trainers also learned how to make the dresses that this Nigerian fashion designer makes so that they could teach with a variety of designs. She wanted her to lead a team that will train over twenty thousand women in six months. The first stage was for her to train the trainers in that country on how to make her style of clothes, then she will supervise them as they teach the women fashion design. That was the beginning of her breakthrough to being a Nigerian multimillionaire, because her contract was extended for another year to train young girls, and then single fathers.

When she returned to Nigeria, the country also awarded her a contract to execute a project like the one she did for widows in the other country. They commended her for representing Nigeria well, and she diligently planned and executed the program in Nigeria. She was able to start her fashion school and accredited it as a continuing education institute. She also allowed her students to apply for employment at her fashion boutique or the school after graduation. In less than three years, she was known as one of the most successful women in the fashion industry and was awarded many honors for mentoring the younger generation, and single mothers.

Meanwhile, on the other side of the world, the boyfriend and his rich wife settled in California. The wife started her graduate education, but she got pregnant before her husband could get any admission into a graduate program. Around the time of her pregnancy, the federal government of Nigeria was auditing the bank account of some politicians and bank managers, and her father was arrested for fraud. So, the government seized all his possessions and requested a freeze on his foreign accounts. Therefore, the daughter was unable to continue her education in the United States. For fear of the unknown, the couple decided to remain in the United States instead of going back to Nigeria. The husband got a job at a warehouse that paid him minimum wage. The wife had the babies, and she secured a job as a cleaner at a hotel. The couple continued to live on minimum wage in California for many years until they were unable to afford rent. They worked ten-hour shifts and barely saw each other because the husband goes to work when the wife gets home at night, and the wife goes to work immediately her husband returns home in the morning. The stress overwhelmed their marriage, and they were contemplating divorce after a few years.

One day, the ex-girlfriend who turned out to be a successful fashion designer was invited to style an American cast for a movie that involved a part of African fusion in California. Since it was her first time in the United States, she decided to take her children along for a vacation. As fate would have it, she lodged at the same hotel where her ex-boyfriend's wife worked as a cleaner. The hotel called for housekeeping to the fashion designer's room, and it was her ex-boyfriend's wife that was asked to go and clean the mess in the room. What a reunion of tears, when she saw her old schoolmate, even though they did not like each other at the university—because they were dating the same man. The fashion designer narrated how much she was heartbroken by her boyfriend, and she had to nurse her twins all by herself. The other lady was very surprised to see the twins because her husband never told her that he continued to date the other girlfriend and impregnated her after graduation. He did this because he had lied to her that he broke up with the less-privileged girl a day before graduation; and that he did not know her whereabouts anymore. He lied to her because he did not want to lose the opportunity to travel to the United States. She also narrated her story about the hardships that they encountered in the United States and that she has a son with the same man. The next day, the wife told her husband about the whole experience that she had at her job the previous night, and she fought him for lying to her. She demanded that the man should go with her to see the ex-girlfriend and apologize. When he saw his ex-girlfriend, he was filled with regrets for underestimating her future based on her poor background. He also regretted not being there as a father for his children, and then he apologized. The ex-girlfriend gracefully accepted his apology and told the couple that she had forgiven them. She even handed them a few hundred dollars and treated them to dinner in the hotel restaurant. The man continually lives with the regret of selling his birthright for a temporary satisfaction of the rich girl's porridge of wealth and American traveling visa. Unfortunately, both wealth and education opportunities are gone. In addition, the visa expired eventually; and his wife abandoned him. Greed is as selfish and deceptive as those who have its qualities— it unexpectedly robs them of the things it gave them earlier.

"What shall it profit a man, if he gained the whole world, but lose his own soul?" (Mark 8:36 King James Version)

12

Get That Bread, Run for The Money

Till very recently, I used to find it funny when I think about the slang, "get that bread;" and I question how bread should be compared to money—bread is just a product of salt, flour, sugar, yeast, and water that you baked in an oven. Why then is bread related to money in a slang? But I realized that bread is one of the most common types of food in the world, and it is almost globalized to the extent that we have to distinguish what kind of bread we are baking. So as I tried to ignore my naïve nature in questioning the reason why bread is used as a reference to money, I concluded that bread has some components that we can relate with some attributes of money— such as yeast that spreads and influences a whole batch of dough—even though only a little quantity of yeast is used in baking bread; salt and sugar that both attract people to its taste and sweetness; and the whole ingredients after being baked will produce carbohydrates that provide the nutritional satisfaction that we all need. Just like sugar, your hard work and prayers may help you get to the peak of your career, but your attitude is the nutritional advantage that will help you stay successful in life. Your character at any position in life is what determines your longevity in that position and would help you accomplish long-term success. The first characteristic that I have noticed in very successful people, who have been rated as prestigious personalities in the society is "humility". Humility is rarely "inbuilt"—we are not born with this trait, but we grow to be humble based on our training or life-changing experiences. An example is my experience as a child. Please do not get me wrong, I am not the humblest individual in the world, and I am still praying to be humble like some of my great friends, whom I admire. I can only use myself in this book as an example because it is easier to narrate my own experience.

Many years ago in Nigeria, I grew up in an environment where the families and friends around me hired domestic staff members to serve them in their homes. As a young girl, I wondered why some of them treated their house helps, drivers, gatekeepers, and other employees like trash. These people are human beings too, and they have a good future that they are working hard towards. My mom made me clean the house and cook with the house help since I was eight years old. The gatemen were my buddies, and the drivers were like my uncles. I had the best childhood ever with all these people, and I will never trade it for anything as an only child. I learned a lot from them, which has helped me to date. Some rich people need to remember the tide always turns, and life changes constantly. They forget the name "Amaechi", which means "who knows tomorrow?" Thanks, mom, for teaching me that you learn priceless lessons when you do not underestimate your teachers. This lesson helped me a lot as I migrated to the United States in my teenage years. I noticed that everyone was treated with respect, regardless of their job position or social status. This helped me to gain favor from people in some circumstances, that you never would have imagined they had the power to help. The tone you use to speak to a customer service agent should be the same tone that you will use to speak to a cleaner, and the same tone you should use to speak to an executive president of a Fortune 500 company. We are all humans with blood and water running in our bodies. There is no difference in the grave for the poor and the rich, so try not to overestimate yourself and look down on anybody else—trust me, it is a challenge for us all. I am also not perfect at this challenge yet like you, but I try to caution myself whenever I notice an unhealthy prideful spirit.

I remember when I did a contract work at an organization in Dallas. I worked till nights a lot because we had a deadline to recover money for the employer. Because of this, I saw the janitors when they came to clean all the desks and our office spaces, and I got acquainted with them. I learned so much from them, more than I ever thought I would learn from college. They were so kind to me, to the extent that they offered to help me move all my things when I was moving to a new home. They came with a truck and moved all my furniture and belongings from my old apartment on multiple trips to my new home, and they did not even allow me to lift a finger to do the work with them. They treated me like a princess, and of course, came to visit with their kids after I settled in. That was one of the greatest positive experiences that I gathered during my contract with that company. I do not know if a lot of my CEO friends might do as much. These are kind acts that even money cannot buy.

Here is something else that I would attribute to success in addition to humility: Always work harder than others while you pray too. Trust me, it pays off. Your prayer can only be answered when you put in some work, as the action of faith. God will not answer a prayer that is not supported by our actions. We always hear that 'Faith without works is dead' (James 2:17 Holman Christian Standard Bible). This reminds me of an African tale that many of us learned from our elders, as an illustration, to work hard, while we pray with faith. I know this tale will help someone too:

> "Once upon a time in a village in Africa, there were two young men who were best friends. They did everything together like brothers and always confided in each other. One day, they decided to go to a fortune-teller who could tell them what would happen to them in the future. The fortune-teller told the first friend that he will be a very rich king; but the second friend was told that he would be extremely poor—no matter how much he tries to succeed. The two friends left the fortune teller and went home to think about the fortune teller's prediction. The first friend said to himself, "I will be rich in the future, so I do not have to work. I will just sit at home to wait for my crown." However, the second friend said to himself. "I was told

that I can never be rich, no matter how much I try. I will go to the forest to start farming on any unoccupied land I see so that I can have food to eat. After all, I might be poor, but I don't want to die hungry". Then the second friend moved to a forest far away from the city. He built a hut to live in; he cleared the grass on a spacious land around his hut; and he planted many fruits, tubers, and vegetables. He continued to live alone in the forest for many years, and he fed himself with the food from his farm. After some years, there was a severe famine in the city, and the people from the city went to the forest in search of food. They saw the farmer and asked if he could kindly give them food to survive. The farmer responded, "I can give you food as much as you want, but you all must make me your king, and you must serve me." The people from the city agreed to that condition, and they moved to the farmer's forest, to serve him. They cleared more land and built more homes around his farm. They paid him taxes and made him their king. One day, the king saw his childhood friend, and he remembered what the fortune teller said in the past. He asked the friend, "Why are you not rich, as the fortune-teller told us?," but his friend responded with regret and many tears, "I was waiting at home for my wealth and crown because the fortune teller said I will be a rich king one day. I did not know that I had to go out to work for my money, then make wealth with the experience and hard work. But you were told otherwise, and you worked hard to avoid the negative predictions against you."

This is one of the best stories that motivate me to work hard for a successful life. What do you think you need to do better today so that you can reach the goals that you set for yourself? Do it, with so much zeal and determination.

About The Author

O lu Laoye (Micaiah) is a recording artist, songwriter, actress, writer, business consultant, entrepreneur, mentor, and motivational speaker. She is also known as 'Micaiah', which has been her musical stage name for several years, with audio songs and music videos that are available on television, radio, and the internet. Her music has reached many in Africa, the United States of America, Europe, and some parts of Asia. She was born in Nigeria, to the late Col. David Bankole Laoye (Rtd), who was the acting state administrator/military governor of the Old Western State in Nigeria; and her mother is Temitayo Taiwo, an international performing artiste. Olu Laoye attributes her talent to her mother's gifts in performing arts, and she was determined to sing and perform like her mother when she heard her mom was given a diplomatic brooch on the day that she performed for President Regan in 1980. Olu believes that if her mother's gifts could open the door to such a big opportunity, then she will emulate her mother's character of embracing her own talents too.

In her teenage years, Olu Laoye migrated with her mother to the United States, where she got her bachelor's degree in International Studies, with concentrations in Peace Studies, Politics, and diplomacy; and she also bagged her Master of Arts degree in Political Science, from the University of North Texas. She is known to have co-published the first quantitative analysis on the relationship between African restorative justice and judicial independence, with Dr. John Ishiyama. She has served on different appointments and on an advisory board, including the board of Advisors at the Southwestern Methodist University Digital Acceleration program, in Dallas, Texas. She also participated in non-profit endeavors in the United States, as the United Nations Association of America's young advocate in Dallas, and Peacemakers in Dallas, Texas. She has a zeal for her Christian music, and charity work. Her biggest goal is to touch many lives positively and to see the success of all those she mentors. She believes all glory is to God, and that is her motto.

Printed in the United States
by Baker & Taylor Publisher Services